THE GRIP OF HONOR: A STORY OF PAUL JONES AND THE AMERICAN REVOLUTION; PP. 1-244

Published @ 2017 Trieste Publishing Pty Ltd

ISBN 9780649597741

The Grip of Honor: A Story of Paul Jones and the American Revolution; pp. 1-244 by Cyrus Townsend Brady

Except for use in any review, the reproduction or utilisation of this work in whole or in part in any form by any electronic, mechanical or other means, now known or hereafter invented, including xerography, photocopying and recording, or in any information storage or retrieval system, is forbidden without the permission of the publisher, Trieste Publishing Pty Ltd, PO Box 1576 Collingwood, Victoria 3066 Australia.

All rights reserved.

Edited by Trieste Publishing Pty Ltd.
Cover @ 2017

This book is sold subject to the condition that it shall not, by way of trade or otherwise, be lent, re-sold, hired out, or otherwise circulated without the publisher's prior consent in any form or binding or cover other than that in which it is published and without a similar condition including this condition being imposed on the subsequent purchaser.

www.triestepublishing.com

CYRUS TOWNSEND BRADY

THE GRIP OF HONOR: A STORY OF PAUL JONES AND THE AMERICAN REVOLUTION; PP. 1-244

Trieste

"It seems to be made out properly and duly signed and sealed," said the captain, slowly.

The Grip of Honor

A Story of Paul Jones and the American Revolution

BY

CYRUS TOWNSEND BRADY

AUTHOR OF "FOR LOVE OF COUNTRY," "FOR THE FREEDOM OF THE SEA," ETC.

> The fear o' Hell's a hangman's whip
> To haud the wretch in order;
> But where ye feel your honor grip,
> Let that aye be your border;
> Its slightest touches, instant pause—
> Debar a' side-pretences;
> And resolutely keep its laws,
> Uncaring consequences.
> — BURNS

NEW YORK
CHARLES SCRIBNER'S SONS
1905

828
B8125g
Q5

Copyright, 1900
By Charles Scribner's Sons

All rights reserved

TO

COLONEL JOHN LEWIS GOOD, U. S. V.,

AND THE OFFICERS AND MEN OF
THE FIRST PENNSYLVANIA UNITED STATES VOLUNTEERS,

MY COMRADES IN THE SPANISH-AMERICAN WAR,

THIS BOOK IS AFFECTIONATELY DEDICATED.

Note

THE interests of the story require some slight variations from exact history in the movements of the Serapis and the Bon Homme Richard before their famous battle, for which the author asks the indulgence of the reader. In all other respects it is believed the account of the battle is sufficiently accurate to present a true picture of the most famous single-ship action ever fought upon the seas.

Contents

Book I

THEY MEET AND PART

CHAPTER		PAGE
I	A STERN CHASE ON A LEE SHORE	3
II	THE CAPTOR CAPTURED	15
III	A GENTLE PIRATE	23
IV	ENTER MAJOR COVENTRY	30
V	SWORDS ARE CROSSED ON THE SAND	38
VI	THE MASTER PLAYER TAKES A HAND	47

Book II

THEY MEET AGAIN

VII	AFTER A LONG TIME	55
VIII	LADY ELIZABETH DOES NOT KNOW THE MARQUIS DE RICHEMONT	66
IX	THE PICTURE ON THE WALL	75
X	LADY ELIZABETH WILL KEEP HER WORD	83
XI	O'NEILL WILL KEEP HIS HONOR	92
XII	GENTLEMEN ALL	106

CONTENTS

Book III

ON THE VERGE OF ETERNITY

Chapter		Page
XIII	A Desperate Move	121
XIV	Almost the End	131
XV	A Soldier and a Gentleman	145

Book IV

THE SELFISHNESS OF LOVE

XVI	In the Line of his Duty	161
XVII	Differing Standards	169

Book V

IN THE HELL OF BATTLE, ALL

XVIII	The Boys in Command	181
XIX	'Tween Decks with the Men	192
XX	The Indomitable Ego	203
XXI	The Audacity of Despair	214
XXII	Sinking, but Triumphant	220

Book VI

THE HAND OF GOD

XXIII	On Board the Serapis Again	229
XXIV	Not Guilty, my Lord	241

Illustrations

"It seems to be made out properly and duly signed and sealed," said the captain, slowly	*Frontispiece*
	TO FACE PAGE
Elizabeth stood with clasped hands, her face pale with emotion, eagerly watching	44
He watched her in awe-struck silence, sank on his knees, stretched out his arms	106
The sharp crack of a musket rang out in the air	166

BOOK I
THEY MEET AND PART

THE GRIP OF HONOR

CHAPTER I

A Stern Chase on a Lee Shore

"THE wind is freshening; we gain upon her easily, I think, sir."

"Decidedly. This is our best point of sailing, and our best wind, too. We can't be going less than ten knots," said the captain, looking critically over the bows at the water racing alongside.

"I can almost make out the name on her stern now with the naked eye," replied the other, staring hard ahead through the drift and spray.

"Have you a glass there, Mr. O'Neill?" asked the captain.

"Yes, sir, here it is," answered that gentleman, handing him a long, old-fashioned, cumbrous brass telescope, which he at once adjusted and focused on the ship they were chasing.

"Ah!" said the elder of the two speakers, a small, slender man, standing lightly poised on the topgallant forecastle with the careless confidence of a veteran seaman, as he examined the chase through the glass which the taller and younger officer handed him; "I can read it quite plainly with this. The M-a-i-d —

THE GRIP OF HONOR

Maidstone, a trader evidently, as I see no gun-ports nor anything that betokens an armament." He ran the tubes of the glass into each other and handed it back, remarking, "At this rate we shall have her in a short time."

"She is a fast one, though," replied the other; "it's no small task for anything afloat to show us her heels for so long a time; let me see — it was six bells in the morning watch when we raised her, was it not, sir?"

"Yes, 'tis rather remarkable going for a merchant vessel, but we have the heels of her and will get her soon unless she goes to the bottom on those reefs round the Land's End yonder. It's a nasty place to be tearing through in that wild way," he added thoughtfully.

"Shall I give her a shot, sir, from the starboard bow-chaser?"

"Not just yet; it would be useless, as we are not quite within range, and she would pay no heed; besides, we shall have her without it, and 'tis hardly worth while wasting a shot upon her at present."

The brief conversation took place forward upon the forecastle of the American Continental ship Ranger, between her captain, John Paul Jones, and her first lieutenant, one Barry O'Neill, Marquis de Richemont, sometime officer in the navy of his Most Christian Majesty, the King of France. O'Neill was the son of a marshal of France, an Irish gentleman of high birth and position, who had gone out as a mere lad with the young Stuart in the '45, and

A STERN CHASE ON A LEE SHORE

whose property had been confiscated, and himself attainted and sentenced to death for high treason. Fortunately he had escaped to the Continent, and had entered the service of the King of France; where, through his extraordinary ability and courage, coupled with several brilliant opportunities he had made and enjoyed, he had risen to exalted station and great wealth. He had always continued more or less of a conspirator in the cause of the royal Stuarts, however, and his son, following in his footsteps, had been mixed up in every treasonable Jacobite enterprise which had been undertaken, and was under the same ban of the British throne as was his father.

When Paul Jones in the historic ship Ranger came to France, O'Neill, moved by a spirit of adventure and his ever present desire to strike a blow at King George, received permission to enter the American service temporarily, with several other French officers. The Ranger was already some days out on her successful cruise, when, early on a morning in the month of April in the year 1778, they had sighted a ship trying to beat around the Land's End. Sail had at once been made in chase, and the stranger was now almost within the grasp of the American pursuers.

"It seems to me, sir," said O'Neill to the captain, "that unless she goes about presently, she won't weather that long reef over beyond her, where those breakers are."

"Ay," said Jones; "and if she goes about, she's ours, and —" He paused significantly

THE GRIP OF HONOR

"If not, sir?"

"She's God's!" added the captain, solemnly.

The wind was blowing at a furious rate. The Ranger had a single reef in her topsails, with her topgallant sails set above them. The masts were straining and buckling like bound giants, and the ship quivered and trembled like a smitten harpstring, as she pitched and plunged in the heavy seas. The wind roaring through the iron-taut rigging, and the wild spray dashing over the sides, rendered conversation almost impossible. The motley crew of the Ranger were gathered forward, clustering on the rail and lower shrouds, keeping of course at a respectful distance from their captain and his first lieutenant, and some of the other officers grouped near them.

"She must tack, now," said Jones at last, "or she's lost. I know these waters; I have sailed them many times when I was a boy. I doubt if they can weather that reef even — By heavens! There's a woman on board of her, too!" he exclaimed, as his keen eye detected the flutter of drapery and a dash of color among a little group of men on the deck of the Maidstone, evidently staring aft at her relentless pursuer.

"See everything in readiness for quick work here. Gentlemen," continued the captain, "to your stations all. Mr. O'Neill, remain with me." The men hastened to their places at once, and a little silence supervened.

"You may give her a shot now, Mr. O'Neill," said Jones at last; "it may bring them to tacking and save

A STERN CHASE ON A LEE SHORE

them from wreck. Pitch it alongside of her; we don't want to hurt the woman, and it's not necessary to touch the ship."

"Clear away that starboard bow-chaser," called the lieutenant; and the men, scarcely waiting for his word of command, cast loose the gun. "Aft there, stand by to give her a touch of the helm!" he cried with raised voice.

"Ay, ay, sir," came the prompt reply.

"Price," continued O'Neill to the captain of the piece, "you need not hit her; just throw a shot alongside of her. Are you ready?"

"All ready, sir," answered the old seaman, carefully shifting his quid and squinting along the gun.

"Luff!" shouted O'Neill, in his powerful voice. The quartermaster put the wheel over a few spokes, and the Ranger shot up into the wind a little and hung quivering a moment with checked way.

"Give her a touch with the right-hand spike, lads," said old Price. "Steady, shove in that quoin a little; easy there, overhaul those tackles! All ready, sir."

"Now!" cried O'Neill.

A booming roar and a cloud of smoke broke out forward, and the ball ricochetted along the water and sank just under the quarter of the chase.

"Let her go off again," cried O'Neill to the quartermaster, and a moment later, as the sails filled and she heeled once more to the wind; "very well dyce, enough off," he cried.

"A good shot, Master Price, and a glass of grog

for you presently in reward," said Jones, quietly "Ah! we shall have some answer, at any rate."

At this moment a small red flag broke out from the gaff of the English vessel.

"Show our own colors aft there, though they can scarcely see them," cried the captain; "he's a plucky one, that fellow. What's he doing now? 'Fore Gad, he's got a gun over the quarter, a stern-chaser. Must have arms on board."

The Ranger was rushing through the water again at a rapidly increasing rate, almost burying her lee cathead in the foaming sea under the freshening breeze, and was now very near the Maidstone, which at this moment discharged the small stern-chaser which had been dragged astern, the shot from which passed harmlessly through the bellying foresail above their heads.

"Give her another, Price," said O'Neill, upon a nod from Jones.

"Into her this time, sir?"

"Yes, anywhere you like."

The Ranger luffed again, losing a little distance as she did so, but weathering appreciably on the stranger, and this time the flying splinters from the stern of the chase showed that the shot had met its mark. There was a sudden scattering of the men upon her quarter, and most of them disappeared, but the young girl could be seen holding on to the weather spanker vang, and apparently looking defiantly at them. O'Neill took up the glass and examined her.

A STERN CHASE ON A LEE SHORE

"Faith, sir, she looks as pretty as she is brave. See for yourself, sir," he added, as he handed the telescope to the captain, who took a careful look at her through the glass.

"You have a good eye for the beautiful," he replied, smiling, "even at a long range. Secure the bow-chaser, sir; we are within musket range of her."

While this was being done, the Ranger had crept up on the stranger till her bow began to overreach the weather quarter of the other vessel. As they held on recklessly together, suddenly the speed of the chase was diminished. Her helm was put down, and with sails quivering and swaying she swung up into the wind.

"We have her now," said Jones, springing on the rail and leaning over forward; "nay, it's too late. Missed stays! By Heaven, she's in irons! She's doomed! Aft there! steady with the helm! Give her a good full."

In the next instant, with a crash heard above the roar of the storm even upon the other ship, the ill-fated Maidstone drove upon the reef broadside on. The shock of meeting was tremendous: her masts were snapped short off like pipe stems; the howling gale jerked them over the sides, where they thundered and beat upon the ship with tremendous force. The girl disappeared.

"Breakers ahead!" on the instant roared out a half-dozen voices in the forecastle.

"Breakers on the starboard bow!" came the wild cry from all sides.

THE GRIP OF HONOR

"Down with the helm, hard down!" shouted O'Neill, with a seaman's ready instinct, without waiting for the captain. There was a moment of confusion on the deck.

"Steady with the helm, steady, sir!" cried Jones, in his powerful voice, with an imperious wave of his hand. "Silence fore and aft the decks! Every man to his station! Keep her a good full, quartermaster. Keep that helm as you have it. Look yonder, sir," he added, pointing to larboard to another danger. "Ready about, stations for stays! Aft with you, Mr. O'Neill, and see that the helm is shifted exactly as I direct. Make no mistake! Lively, men, for your lives!"

The eager crew sprang to their stations. There was another moment or two of confusion; and as they settled down, the silence was broken only by the wind and the waves. The water was seething and whirling under the forefoot of the Ranger. The reefs upon which the Maidstone had crashed were dangerously near. But the keen eye of the captain had seen on the other side a slender needle of rock over which the waves broke in seething fury as it thrust itself menacingly out of the angry ocean. They were right among the reefs, and only the most complete knowledge and consummate seamanship could save them. It was there.

To tack ship now and come up in the wind would throw them on the rocky needle; to go off would bring them down upon the other reefs. Jones, entirely master of the situation, perfectly cool in appear-

A STERN CHASE ON A LEE SHORE

ance, though his eyes snapped and sparkled with fire, leaned out above the knightheads and keenly scanned the sea before him. There was just room for the Ranger to pass between the two reefs. A hair's breadth on either side would mean destruction. As the captain watched the boiling water he seemed to detect, through a slight change in the course, a tremor in the hand on the wheel.

"Aft there!" he shouted promptly, "what are you about? Steady with that helm! No higher — nothing off!"

"Ay, ay, sir," replied O'Neill, standing watchfully at the con; "I will mind it myself."

The crash of the breakers, as they writhed their white-crested heads around the ship's bows and on either side, was appalling to every one. They were right in them now — passing through them. The rocky needle on the larboard hand slipped by and drew astern. The wreck of the Maidstone was lost sight of in the flooding waves and driving spray of a rising gale. The ship was roaring through the seas at a terrific rate; the strain upon everything was tremendous; a broken spar, a parted rope, meant a lost ship.

"Very well dyce," cried the captain, casting a glance aloft at the weather leech of the topsails shivering in the fierce wind, the quivering masts and groaning yard-arms, the lee shrouds hanging slack, the lee braces and head bowlines taut as strung wires, the tacks and sheets and the weather shrouds as rigid as iron bars, the new canvas like sheets of marble. The ship was heeled over until the lee channels were almost awash, the spray coming in, in bucketsful, over the lee cathead. She was ready if ever she would be; their fate was at the touch.

"Now!" shouted Jones, in a voice of thunder "Down with the helm! Over with it! Hard over!"

The old experienced seamen put the wheel over spoke by spoke, slowly at first, then faster, until they finally hauled it down hard and clung to it with all the strength of their mighty arms.

"Helm's-a-lee, hard-a-lee," cried O'Neill at this moment.

"Rise tacks and sheets," roared the captain.

The ship shot up into the wind, straightened herself as its pressure was removed from the sails, lost headway, the jibs swinging and tugging in the gale, as she began to swing to larboard away from the reef on the starboard side. She worked around slowly until the wind began to come in over the starboard bow.

"Haul taut!" shouted the watching captain; "mainsail haul!"

The great yards, with their vast expanse of slatting, roaring, threshing canvas, whirled rapidly around as the nimble crew ran aft with the sheets and braces. The Ranger fell off quickly and drifted down toward the needle, the aftersails aback.

"Board that main tack there! Man the head braces; jump, men, lively! Let go and haul!"

There was a frightful moment, — would she make

A STERN CHASE ON A LEE SHORE

it? She stopped — Ah, thank God, they gathered way again, slowly, then faster.

"Right the helm! Meet her — so. Steady! Get that main tack down now, tail on to it, all of you, sway away! Get a pull on the lee braces, Mr. O'Neill, and haul the bowlines. Ah! That's well done."

They were rushing through it again; the white water and the breakers were left behind. A sigh of relief broke from the reckless men, and even the iron captain seemed satisfied with his achievement as he walked aft to the quarter-deck.

"Get a good offing, Mr. O'Neill," said the captain, "and then heave to. First send the hands aloft to take in the to'gallant sails, and then you may get a boat ready; we must see if there are any poor creatures left on that ship yonder."

"Very good, sir," replied the lieutenant, giving the necessary orders, when presently the ship, easier under the reduced canvas, was hove to in the beating sea.

"Shall I take the weather whaleboat, sir?"

"Yes," returned the captain, "I think you would better try to board under her lee if it be possible to do anything among that wreckage. I doubt if there be anybody left alive on her, but we can't afford to risk the possibility, especially in the case of that woman whom you found so beautiful," he added with a smile.

"Ay, ay, sir," said the lieutenant, blushing beneath the bronze in spite of himself, as he directed the boatswain to call away the whaleboat, which, manned by six stout oarsmen, with himself at the tiller, was soon cast into the heaving sea. Meanwhile the Ranger filled away again and beat to and fro off the coast, taking care to preserve the necessary offing, or distance from shore to leeward.

CHAPTER II

The Captor Captured

IT was a long hard pull, and only the great skill of the officer prevented their capsizing, before the whaleboat finally drew near the Maidstone. The ship had hit the reef hard at flood-tide, and the waves had driven her farther on. Every mast and spar was gone, wrenched away by the storm and the waves. It was manifestly impossible to approach upon the weather side without staving the boat, so O'Neill cautiously rounded the stern of the wreck, and briefly considered the situation.

He did not dare bring the boat near enough to enable him to leap upon the deck through some of the great gaping openings in the sides made by the tremendous battering of the massive spars, and he finally concluded that the only practicable access to the Maidstone was by means of some of the gearing trailing over the side and writhing about snake-like in the water. Intrusting the tiller of the whaleboat to old Price, the veteran gunner, he directed that it be brought alongside as close as consistent with safety; and at exactly the right moment, as they rose upon the crest of a wave, he sprang out into the water, and clutched desperately at a rope hanging over the side of the wreck.

THE GRIP OF HONOR

The men swung the boat away from the ship instantly, and he found himself clinging to a small rope wildly tossing about in the tumultuous sea. He was dashed to and fro like a cork, the waves repeatedly broke over his head, the life was almost buffeted out of him, but he held on like grim death. Fortunately, the other end of the rope was fast inboard.

With careful skill, and husbanding his strength as much as possible, he pulled himself along the rope through the water until he drew near the side of the ship. Then, though the operation was hazardous in the extreme, as he saw no other method, he began to pull himself up hand over hand on the rope along the side. In his already exhausted state and with the added weight of his wet, sodden clothing, the effort was almost beyond his strength.

He endeavored by thrusting with his foot to keep himself from being beaten against the side by the waves, but without success, for when he had hardly reached the rail, an unusually large breaker struck him fairly in the back and dashed his head against a piece of jagged timber, cutting a great gash in his forehead. Blood filled his eyes, his head swam, a sick, faint feeling filled his breast, he hesitated and nearly lost his grasp of the rope. The men in the tossing boat a little distance away held their breath in terrified apprehension, but summoning all his resolution to his aid, he made a last desperate effort, breasted the rail, and fell fainting prone upon the deck of the ship.

A few moments in the cold water which was flood-

THE CAPTOR CAPTURED

ing over it revived him somewhat, and he rose unsteadily to his feet, and looked about him in bewilderment. The change from the tossing boat to the motionless rigidity of the vise-held wreck was startling. There was not a sign of life on the ship. She was breaking up fast; rails were stove in, boats were gone, three jagged stumps showed where the masts had been, and only the fact that she had been driven so high on the reefs prevented her from foundering at once. There was a dead body jammed under the starboard fife-rail forward, but no other sign of humanity. In front of him was a hatchway, giving entrance to a small cuddy, or cabin, the roof of which rose a few feet above the level of the deck.

As he stood there, striving to recover himself, in a brief lull in the storm he thought he heard a faint voice; it seemed to come from beneath him. He at once turned, and with uncertain steps descended the hatchway. Reaching the deck below, he stood in the way a moment, brushing the blood from his eyes. As he gradually made out the details of the cabin, dimly illuminated by a skylight above, he saw a woman on her knees praying; she had her face buried in her hands, and did not see him until he spoke to apprise her of his presence.

"Madam," he began thickly.

The woman raised her head with startled quickness, and gave him one terrified glance. The glass had told him truly, — she was beautiful, and young as well, scarcely more than a girl apparently; even the dim gray light could not hide those things. As for him, he was an awful-looking spectacle: wet, hatless, his clothing torn, a great red wound in his forehead intensifying his pallor. He had a heavy pistol in his belt and a cutlass swinging at his side.

She stared at him in frightened silence and finally rose to her feet deathly pale and apparently appalled; he saw that she was a little above the medium height. At the same moment, from an obscure corner, there rang out shriek after shriek, and another woman rushed forward, threw herself on the deck at his feet and fairly grovelled before him.

"Oh, sir, for God's sake, sir," she cried frantically, "good mister pirate, don't hang us, sir! We never hurt nobody. Oh, sir, take us away, we'll do anything, we —"

"Silence, you coward!" commanded the other woman, imperiously. "Get up! Prayers are of no avail with such as —"

"Nor are they necessary, madam," replied O'Neill; "we are not pirates, and I am come to save you and shall do it. Will you please come on deck?"

"I had rather gone down on the ship," said the girl, defiantly, evidently disbelieving him; "but you are here, and you are master. Give your orders, sir."

"Very well," returned the lieutenant, calmly accepting the situation; "you will go up on deck at once." The girl motioned him forward.

"After you, madam," he said, bowing courteously, and she stepped haughtily up the companion-way,

THE CAPTOR CAPTURED

followed next by her shivering, shrinking, terrified maid, and lastly by O'Neill.

"Are there any others left alive on the ship, think you, madam?" he asked.

"No one," answered the girl; "many were thrown overboard or killed when we struck on these rocks here, and the rest abandoned us — the cowards," was the reply.

"Do you wait here a moment, while I take a look forward to assure myself," said O'Neill, stepping rapidly across the raffle of rope about the decks, and making a hasty inspection to make sure that no unfortunate was left. Quickly satisfying himself that they were alone, he returned to the quarter-deck where the two women stood. He looked at them in some perplexity. It would be a matter of great difficulty to get them back in the boat, but he promptly determined upon his course of action; they would not like it, but that would be no matter.

Signing to the coxswain, old Price, the boat which had been riding to a long rope from the ship was skilfully brought alongside again as near as was safe. One end of a long piece of loose gear was thrown over to the boat, where it was made fast. A bight of the rope, properly stoppered to prevent undue constriction, was passed around the waist of the maid, at which all her terrors were resumed.

"Oh, for God's sake, sir, for the love of Heaven, as you have a mother or wife, do not hang us here! If we must die, let us drown on the ship like good Christian people. Oh, please, good mister pirate—"

But O'Neill was in no mood to pay attention to such trifling, and he summarily fastened the bight around her waist, and lifting her upon the rail, bade her jump. She clung to him with the tenacity of despair, crying and shrieking in the most frantic manner, until finally her overwrought nerves gave way, and she fainted. That was just what he wanted. Singing out to old Price to haul in on the line, and having taken a turn around a belaying pin with his end of it, he promptly threw the girl into the water. Of course she was dragged under at once, but in a moment was lifted safely into the whaleboat, where she was shortly revived from unconsciousness by the ducking she had received.

"Now, madam, you see you need fear nothing," said O'Neill, peremptorily, to the other woman. "I trust I shall not be compelled to throw you in, too?"

"Not at all, sir," she replied trembling violently, but striving to preserve her self-control; "I presume you reserve me for a worse fate."

The young lieutenant started violently at the insult, and his face clouded darkly at her suspicion.

"I — no matter, I came to save you," he said, as he stepped toward her to assist her to make the leap.

"Please do not touch me," she answered disdainfully; "I am no fainting fool. Give me the rope. What is it you wish me to do?"

"Pass it around your waist. Allow me. Now stand there, madam, and when I say the word, jump!"

"Very well," she said, stepping upon the rail re-

THE CAPTOR CAPTURED

signedly, where perforce he was compelled to hold her to keep her from falling.

How glorious and splendid she looked, he thought, with her unbound hair floating like golden sunlight in the wind against the background of the gray day, while her sea-blue eyes looked boldly over the black water from her proud, white, handsome face.

"Now!" he said, as the boat rose toward them. Without a moment's hesitation, she leaped into the air, and after a swift passage through the water she was hauled into the boat by the rough but kindly hands of the old sailor. Making the end of the rope fast around his own waist, O'Neill, watching his opportunity, sprang after; but he seemed fated for misfortune that day, for a bit of timber torn that moment from the wreck struck him in the head just as he touched the water, and it was a fainting, senseless man Price hauled into the boat. The old seaman laid his officer down in the stern-sheets where the young girl was sitting with her maid crouching at her feet. Necessarily he lay in a constrained position,—there was nothing to support his head but a boat-stretcher.

She gazed upon his pallid face with its disfiguring wounds; he was a murderous pirate, no doubt, and deserved it all, still he had saved her life; the Maidstone was breaking up; he was so handsome too, and he looked like a gentleman. She was a woman, well—then the womanly instincts of the girl asserted themselves, and she finally moved her position and lifted the head of the unconscious sailor to her knee.

THE GRIP OF HONOR

Taking a handkerchief from her neck, she dipped it in the salt water and bathed his head and then poured between his lips a few drops from the flask of rum which Price handed her, after the old man had insisted that she take a draught of the fiery liquid herself.

Under these pleasant ministrations O'Neill opened his eyes for a moment, gazed up into her face with a smiling glance, and closing his eyes immediately, lest she should release him, he lay quite still while the men pulled away toward the Ranger, and in that manner they reached her side. His heart was beating wildly; that look had been enough. She was his prisoner — but her captor was captured!

CHAPTER III

A Gentle Pirate

EAGER eyes on the ship had noted the every movement of the whaleboat as she drew near the Ranger. Old Price saw that a whip and a boatswain's chair had been rigged on the main-yard-arm to swing his passengers on board. The sight of the dangling rope awakened a fresh fit of apprehension on the part of the timorous maid, and it was with great difficulty that the amused seaman persuaded her that she was not to be hanged outright. Entirely unconvinced, but resigning herself to her fate, she finally sat down on the small board and was swung to the gangway.

Her mistress gently laid the head of the prostrate officer against one of the thwarts, and, leaving the handkerchief as a rest for it, followed the maid. Then the old coxswain secured the lieutenant to the chair, and when he had reached the deck, where he opened his eyes and recovered consciousness with incredible promptness, the boat was dropped astern, the falls hooked on, and she was smartly run up to her place at the davits, and the Ranger filled away. O'Neill was at once assisted below to his cabin, and his wounds, which were not serious, were attended to by the surgeon.

THE GRIP OF HONOR

When the young woman joined her maid on the deck, her glance comprehended a curious picture. In front of her, hat in hand, bowing low before her, stood a small, dapper, swarthy, black-avised, black-haired man, in the blue uniform of a naval officer. He had the face of a scholar and a student, with the bold, brilliant, black eyes of a fighter. Surrounding him were other officers and several young boys similarly dressed. Scattered about in various parts of the ship, as their occupation or station permitted, were a number of rude, fierce, desperate-looking men, nondescript in apparel. None of the navies of the world at that date, except in rare instances, uniformed its men. On either side of the deck black guns protruded through the ports, and here and there a marine, carrying a musket and equipped in uniform of white and green, stood or paced a solitary watch.

"I bid you welcome to my ship, madam; so fair a face on a war-vessel is as grateful a sight as the sun after a squall," said the officer, elaborately bowing.

"Sir," said the young woman, trembling slightly, "I am a person of some consideration at home. My guardian will cheerfully pay you any ransom if you spare me. I am a woman and alone. I beg you, sir, to use me kindly;" she clasped her hands in beseeching entreaty, her beautiful eyes filling with tears.

At this signal the fears of the maid broke out afresh, and she plumped down on her knees and

A GENTLE PIRATE

grasped the captain around the legs, bawling vociferously, and adding a touch of comedy to the scene.

"Oh, sir, for the love of Heaven, sir, don't make us walk the plank!" It would seem that the maid had been reading romances.

The seamen near enough to hear and see grinned largely at this exhibition, and the captain, with a deep flush and a black frown on his face, struggled to release himself.

"Silence, woman!" he cried fiercely, at last. "Get up from your knees, or, by Heaven, I will have you thrown overboard; and you, madam, for what do you take me?"

"Are you not a — a pirate, sir?" she answered, hesitating. "They told me on the ship that you — "

"No pirate am I," interrupted the man, proudly, laying his hand on his sword. "I am an officer, and, with these gentlemen, am in the service of the United States of America, the new Republic — this is the American Continental ship Ranger. You are as safe with us as you would be in your own parlor at home. Safer, in fact; there you would be surrounded by servants; here are men who would die to prevent harm coming to you — Is it not so, gentlemen?"

A deep chorus of "Ay, ay's" rang through the air. The captain continued with sudden heat, —

"'Fore God, madam, I don't understand how you could insult me with an offer of money!"

"Oh, sir," said the girl, visibly relieved, "they

told me that you were a pirate, and would murder us all. Are you not — "

"Captain John Paul Jones, at your service, madam," interrupted the little officer, with another bow, thrusting his hand in his bosom.

"Yes," said the young woman; "they said it would be you. Why, every news-letter in the land describes you as — as — "

"Pirate, madam, say it; you have not hesitated to speak the word heretofore. A rebel — a traitor — a pirate," he said, throwing up his head proudly, — "'t is a penalty which one pays for fighting for freedom; but you, at least, shall be able to speak unequivocally as to our character, for I pledge you my word you shall take no harm from us, though I doubt not my young gentlemen here will be raked fore and aft by the batteries of your bright eyes. Now will you vouchsafe me your name and some of your story, that I may know with whom I have to do?"

"My name is Howard, sir, — Elizabeth Howard," replied the girl, brightening as her fears diminished. "I am the ward of Admiral Lord Westbrooke, the governor of Scarborough Castle. I have no father nor mother."

"Another claim upon our consideration, ma'am."

"Sir, I thank you. I was going to visit friends in Liverpool when that unfortunate ship there was wrecked. Oh, what will become of me now?" she exclaimed, her eyes filling with tears again.

"Liverpool lies in our way, Mistress Howard, and

A GENTLE PIRATE

't will give me great pleasure to land you upon some convenient point on the coast in a few days if the wind hold, and no mischance arise; and now may I present my officers to you, since we are to be fellow-passengers all."

Upon receiving the desired permission from the grateful girl, in whose pale cheek the color began to come again, the captain, who was a great stickler for etiquette, brought forward the little group of officers and introduced them one by one. There was much bowing and courtesying on the quarter-deck, which even the seamen seemed to enjoy.

"This is all, I believe," said the captain, having stopped with the smallest midshipman, who announced himself in his boyish treble, in comical imitation of his elders, as, "vastly honored, madam."

"The gentleman who brought me here?" questioned the girl, blushing faintly; "I trust he is not seriously injured?"

"Ah!" replied Jones, "my first lieutenant, Mr. Barry O'Neill, a volunteer with us, and an officer in the service of his most Christian Majesty, my friend, the King of France." On the ship O'Neill had elected to sink his marquisate.

"He is not much hurt, Mistress Howard, only battered about a bit and pulled down by the nervous shock and efforts he underwent — why, here he is now! Did I not warn you, sir, to stay below?" said the doctor, shaking his finger, as O'Neill, pale and languid, with his head bound up, came slowly up the companion-way.

"Oh, I am all right, doctor," said the lieutenant, rather weakly, but smiling with the audacity and gallantry of his race as he spied the girl. "Who would stay below with divinity on the deck? The thought of the presence of this lady above him would lift a crusader from his tombstone."

"Allow me to present you in due form to Mistress Howard, Mr. O'Neill," said the captain, somewhat severely, evidently very desirous of observing the proprieties now.

"Sir," said the young girl, looking gratefully at the Irishman out of her violet eyes, "I have to thank you for a most gallant rescue, made doubly hard by my perversity and foolish apprehension, which this gentleman," bowing to the flattered captain, "has most kindly removed."

"'T was a pleasure to serve you, madam. May I continue to enjoy it. We would sink another ship for such another chance," said the Irishman, lightly.

"Now I propose to give up one of my cabins to Mistress Howard and her maid," said the captain; "and I presume that she will need to rest after the exciting incidents of the day until supper is served. If you are able, Mr. O'Neill, I should like to have you join us there, with Mistress Howard's permission, of course, since the ship is hers." He smiled toward her, and when he smiled he was irresistible.

"I am honored, sir," replied the girl, graciously. "And I thank you. Captain, I shall be delighted," continued the young lady, laying her hand in his own, as he led her aft to the cabin door in the break

A GENTLE PIRATE

of the poop. Before she entered, she turned and made a graceful courtesy; her glance swept toward the young lieutenant — O'Neill from that moment was no longer a captive — he was a slave.

"Gentlemen, good-afternoon," she said, comprehending them in one brilliant look, and smiling again — it was enough; that glance had given O'Neill any number of rivals.

CHAPTER IV

Enter Major Coventry

THREE days later the Ranger, under all plain sail, in a gentle breeze, was slowly ploughing along through the Irish Sea, off the English coast, near the mouth of the Mersey. The whaleboat, manned by six of the smartest seamen, armed with cutlass and pistol, and dressed in their best clothes, old Price being coxswain again, was just being made ready. The ship was presently hove to, and a side ladder was dropped overboard at the gangway where Miss Elizabeth Howard and her maid were standing waiting for the lowering of the whaleboat, and around which the officers of the deck speedily congregated.

They were a sorrowful lot of men, these impressionable sailors, for O'Neill was not alone in his captivity. True to his promise, Captain Jones had shifted his course, and was about to land his fair passenger. He had chosen to put her ashore upon a rocky beach four or five miles away from a fort at Birkenhead, which guarded the mouth of the river which gave entrance to the harbor, not caring to venture his ship in any closer proximity to the fortifications and the war-vessels probably in the river.

ENTER MAJOR COVENTRY

It was a risky performance at best, but he trusted to the known speed of the Ranger and his own seamanship to effect his escape in case the ship should be discovered and pursued in force.

Once on shore, it would not be a difficult matter for the lady and her maid to procure a conveyance to take them to the city a little farther inland. The melancholy duty of landing the two women, by special request, had been allotted to the first lieutenant, much to the disgust of the various midshipmen who conceived that the matter of taking charge of boats appertained more properly to one of their number.

The farewells were soon spoken by the grateful girl to the officers, who had done their very best in making the days pass pleasantly and lightening the tedium of the voyage, and to the captain, who had been kindness and consideration itself. The young lieutenant, still somewhat pale from his adventure, had clothed himself in a handsome full-dress uniform, and, with a splendidly jewelled sword swinging by his side, came on deck from his cabin, the envy of all the others.

The ship had been hove to, the accommodation ladder shipped, the whaleboat was lying at the gangway now, and the three passengers at once took their places in the stern.

"See Miss Howard safely landed, Mr. O'Neill," said the solicitous captain, leaning over the rail, "and assure yourself, as far as possible, of her ability to reach the town without harm, and then return at once; in any event, do not leave the beach. We will watch you, sir."

"Ay, ay, sir," answered O'Neill. "Shove off — out oars — give way!" and the little boat at once shot away from the side, and, under the impetus given by the watchful men, dashed toward the not distant shore.

Miss Howard should have been radiantly happy at leaving the Ranger, and in her proximity to Liverpool, where she was about to meet not only friends and family connections, but one who was destined to be something more. This person was Major Edward Coventry, a gallant and distinguished young officer, the son and heir of her guardian, Lord Westbrooke, and to whom for many years — from infancy, in fact — she had been betrothed. But an unaccountable tinge of sadness hovered over her lovely face, though she strove to conceal it under an affectation of lightness and gayety.

As for O'Neill, he made no effort whatever to hide his misery. The impressionable young Irishman had fallen deeply in love with Elizabeth Howard. He had fallen in love a thousand times before, but not in this way; and the heart which had withstood the successful assaults of the brilliant beauties of the gay court of France had literally succumbed at the first sight of this beautiful English girl whom benignant fortune had thrown across his path.

She, and she only, was his fate, then and thereafter. A new and hitherto unknown feeling had been excited in his heart at the sight of her. In

ENTER MAJOR COVENTRY

that hour in the boat when he lay with his head upon her knee, when he had looked up at her, heaven had opened before his gaze, and to his disordered fancy she had seemed an angel. Each passing moment discovered in her a new charm, and he loved her with the impetuosity of a boy, the doting passion of an old man, and the consecration of a devotee.

With the daring of his race, he had not hesitated to acquaint the girl with his passion, either, though it was stale news to her; there is nothing a woman discovers more quickly and more certainly than the feelings of a man who loves her. That she had laughed at his ardor had not in the least deterred him from persisting in his attentions, which she had not found unwelcome, for he thoroughly understood the value of determined pursuit. She had told him that they were like two ships sailing the great sea, whose paths happened to cross for a moment. They meet, nod to each other, and pass on; the deep swallows them up, and they see each other no more forever.

He had vowed and protested that it would not be so; that England was a little country and Admiral Westbrooke a great man; that she could not be anywhere without attracting the attention of the world, — she could by no means hide her light; that he would withdraw from the American service, which he could honorably do at the expiration of the present cruise, and search the whole island until he found her, — all of which was pleasant for her to hear, of course, though it elicited no more favorable reply. She was attracted to the young man: his handsome person, his cultured mind, his charming manners were such that no one — no woman, that is — could be indifferent to them; but she did not love him, at least not yet.

Elizabeth Howard was a woman to make a man fall desperately in love with her, and many men had done so. She was tall and graceful, golden-haired, blue-eyed, and of noble presence. She was proud, she was wise, she was witty, she was tender, she was contemplative, she was gay, she was sad, she was joyous, in different moods. Days, years even, could not exhaust the charms of her infinite variety, though far down beneath the surface of her nature were the quiet deeps of constancy and devotion, — what plummet could sound them, who should discover them? There was about her that indefinable air of one born for homage and command which speaks of generations to whom have been accorded honor and place unquestioned.

It was not a long row to the land; and as they approached the rugged coast, the young lieutenant eagerly scanned the shore for a landing-place. Steering around a little promontory which hid them from the Ranger, he discovered a stretch of sandy beach under its lee, and the boat was sent in its direction until the keel grated on the soft sand. It was a lonely spot, a little stretch of sand ending inland, and on one side in precipitous rocks over which a wandering pathway straggled unevenly to

ENTER MAJOR COVENTRY

the heights above. The other end of the beach gave entrance, through a little opening, or pass in the rocks, upon a country road which wandered about inland, losing itself under some trees a mile or so away.

On the rocky promontory back of, and at one end of the beach, there was a small lighthouse; and several miles from the beach in the other direction, at the end of the road probably, was a castle or fort, the flag floating lazily from the staff indicating that it was garrisoned. Springing lightly from the boat, O'Neill stepped recklessly into the water alongside. Miss Howard rose to her feet and looked anxiously about her.

"Allow me," said O'Neill; and then, without waiting for permission, he lifted her gently in his arms and carried her to the shore. "Would that all the earth were water, and that I might carry you forever," he said, as he put her down upon the sand.

"You would not like heaven, then?" she replied, jesting.

"I find my present experience of it delightful, madam; but why do you say that?" he asked anxiously.

"Because there, we are told, there will be no more sea!" she answered with well-simulated gayety.

"'T is a poor place for a sailor, then," he replied gravely, in no mood for badinage, "and I fear few of them will get there."

Price, who had followed his officer's example with

the maid, now stepped up to him for his orders, necessarily interrupting the conversation.

"Price," he said to that intrepid old sailor, "you may go back to the boat and shove off, and keep her under the lee of that little point until I call you. Keep a sharp lookout, too."

"Ay, ay, sir," said the old sailor, turning to fulfil the command.

"Now I suppose the time has come for me to say good-bye to Lieutenant O'Neill," said Elizabeth.

"Oh, not yet, Miss Howard; I cannot leave you here alone until I know that you are safe."

"But your duty, sir?"

"A gentleman's, a sailor's, first duty is always toward a helpless woman, especially if she is —"

"His prisoner, you would say, I suppose?" she said, interrupting hastily. That was not at all what he had intended to say, but he let it pass.

"You know who is prisoner, now and forever, Miss Howard."

"If you refer to Lieutenant O'Neill, I will release him now and forever as well, at once, sir," she said archly.

"You cannot."

"As you will, sir," she replied; "but as I happen to see several horsemen coming down the road yonder, I imagine you will not be detained from your ship a very long time. Let us go forward to meet them; perhaps they can give us some information."

The horsemen, evidently an officer and two order-

ENTER MAJOR COVENTRY

lies who were galloping toward the beach, at this moment noticed the boat party and probably the Ranger itself. They reined in their horses at once, and the officer apparently gave some directions to one of the others, for he saluted, turned his horse about in the road, and galloped rapidly back in the direction of the castle. The officer then trotted hastily forward, followed by the remaining man, and looking intently ahead of him until he reached the vicinity of the little group, he dismounted, and handing the bridle to the soldier, bade him wait where he was. He came forward fearlessly, with one hand on his sword, the other holding a pistol which he had taken from the holster. He was a young and handsome man in a new and brilliant scarlet uniform.

CHAPTER V

Swords are Crossed on the Sand

"LADY ELIZABETH, you here?" he exclaimed, stopping short in great surprise, when he was near enough to recognize them. "What is the meaning of this?" He stood a moment as if petrified, and then came nearer. "Who is this person?" he demanded imperiously. Elizabeth started violently.

"Major Coventry! Edward!" she cried.

"Are you a 'Lady,' madam?" said O'Neill, in equal surprise, addressing the astonished girl and paying no attention to the officer.

"For what else do you take her, sir?" interrupted the officer, bristling with indignation.

"Faith, sir, I would take her 'for better or worse,' an I could," replied the Irishman, smiling.

"Unfortunately for you, that is a privilege I propose to exercise myself," said the Englishman, sternly.

"The world will doubtless share my regret, sir," said the Irishman, audaciously, a bitter pang in his breast at this unlooked for news.

"Now I wish to know who you are and how you come here and what you are doing,—an explanation, sir!" asked the officer.

SWORDS ARE CROSSED ON THE SAND

"I am not accustomed to give explanations save to those who have the right to demand them," replied O'Neill.

"I have two rights, sir."

"They are?"

"First, I am betrothed to this young lady," said the officer. "Second, this," laying his hand upon his sword.

"Either of these may be sufficient from your point of view, neither of them from mine. As to the first, I refer you to the young lady herself: I will have it from her own lips, or not at all; as to the second, you will see I have a similar right of my own."

"Will you, Lady Elizabeth," said the young officer, addressing her formally, "have the goodness to inform me how you came here and who this person is, or shall I force the knowledge from him?"

"If you wish him to have the information, Miss Howard, you would, I think, better give it him. Otherwise I do not see how he is to get it," said O'Neill, grimly, his dark face flushing with anger.

"This gentleman," said the girl, faintly, pointing to the officer, "is Major Edward Coventry, the son of my guardian, Admiral Westbrooke."

"And your betrothed, Elizabeth; you forget that," added Coventry.

"I almost wish I could," she replied sharply, gathering courage. "You remind me of it too constantly for it to be pleasant, and at no time so inopportunely as at the present."

The Englishman, in great astonishment and per-

THE GRIP OF HONOR

turbation, opened his mouth to speak, but he was interrupted by the quicker Irishman.

"Why so, Mistress Howard?"

"Lady Elizabeth, if you please, sir," said Coventry.

"Lady Elizabeth, then. I thank you, sir, for the reminder," answered O'Neill, suavely. "Your friends on the Ranger are all interested in your welfare, and I am sure they are glad in my person to meet with and congratulate the fortunate gentleman who aspires to your hand." He smiled bitterly at her as he spoke.

"Will you tell me or not, Lady Elizabeth, who this person is and how you came here?" said Coventry, impatiently, with mounting choler at all this by-play.

"This is a lieutenant of the American Continental ship Ranger, Captain John Paul Jones——"

"The d——d, murdering pirate!" exclaimed Coventry, hotly.

"Stop!" cried O'Neill, stepping forward with his hand upon his sword. "You shall neither swear before a lady, nor shall you in this scandalous manner disparage the ship of which I have the honor to be the first lieutenant, nor asperse the character of her captain. Withdraw your words, or you shall answer to me with that which hangs by your side."

"I fight only with gentlemen," said Coventry, coldly.

"My custom," replied O'Neill, promptly, "is in the main the same as your own; but I sometimes make exceptions, which I am willing to do in this instance. I require you immediately, instantly, to apologize to me for your remarks."

SWORDS ARE CROSSED ON THE SAND

"And if I refuse?"

"I shall strike them down your throat with my hand."

"'S death, sir! How dare you, a beggarly adventurer, talk thus to me, an officer, a major in the army of his Gracious Majesty King George, a Coventry, a Westbrooke!"

"If you were an angel from heaven 't would make no difference to me, for I would have you know, sir, that I am of as good a house as — ay, a better than — your own, a descendant of kings —"

"An Irishman, I infer?" said Coventry, sneering.

"You are correct, sir, and my people have been chieftains for thirty generations."

"Ah, in Ireland?" The manner of the question made it another insult, but O'Neill restrained himself under the great provocation and answered coldly:

"Where else, sir, and where better? As for me, I am temporarily an officer of yonder ship, the Ranger, flying the flag of the American Republic, but I am a lieutenant in the navy of his Majesty Louis XVI. My father is a marshal of France. Will you draw now?" he cried, stepping forward impetuously.

"A brilliant array of titles surely; pity it lacks other confirmation than your word. I scarcely comprehend the catalogue," replied Coventry, coldly.

"I shall endeavor to enlighten you as to my credibility with this," said O'Neill, drawing his sword. "Now will you fight or not?"

"And if I persist in my refusal?" asked Coventry, who was playing for time.

"At this juncture I shall be under the painful necessity of killing you in the presence of your betrothed, so draw, my dear sir, if not for honor, for —"

"What?"

"Life!"

"On guard!" cried the Englishman, whipping out his sword.

"Stop!" cried Elizabeth, springing between their swords. "He saved my life at the risk of his own."

"D — n him!" said the Englishman, grinding his teeth.

"Your condemnation comes too late, sir," said O'Neill, with bitter emphasis, with an expressive glance at Elizabeth, who continued impetuously:

"This gentleman treated me with the most distinguished courtesy."

"I wish that he had exhibited some of it here," interrupted Coventry again.

"I have but followed your own example," retorted O'Neill, calmly.

"Will you hear me in silence, Edward? They are not pirates —"

"I call them so," said Coventry, stubbornly.

"Enough, Lady Elizabeth," said O'Neill, taking his share in the conversation again. "Two lovers are sometimes an embarrassment of riches. This seems to be one of the times. If you will stand aside, I trust that a few moments will rid you of one or the other of them."

"I will not go!" said the girl, defiantly. "You shall not fight; you have nothing to quarrel about."

SWORDS ARE CROSSED ON THE SAND

"We have you, or rather he has," responded the Irishman.

"Withdraw, I beg of you, Elizabeth. This matter must be settled," said Coventry, in his turn.

"I will not, I tell you!" persisted the girl, determinedly. "If you fight, you will fight through me."

"We are doing that now," said O'Neill, savagely. "Will you withdraw, madam?"

"I repeat it, I will not, and I wish to remind you that I do not like your tone. You are not on the deck of your ship now, sir."

"Oh, am I not? Boat ahoy, there! Price," cried O'Neill, waving his hand. A few strokes brought the whaleboat to the shore again. The crew were eager to take a hand in the fray. "Coxswain, come here," said the officer.

"Ay, ay, sir," replied the sailor; and while the other two stood wondering, the veteran seaman rolled up to them and saluted his lieutenant with a sea scrape. "Want us to take a hand in this yere little scrimmage, yer Honor?"

"No. Take this lady and her maid to that clump of rocks yonder."

"That's easy; 'tain't no fightin' at all, that. Come along, yer Leddyship," said the old man, in great disappointment, as the boat shoved off again.

"You monster!" cried Elizabeth, stamping her foot on the sand. "You are a pirate, after all!"

"As you say, madam. Stop, sir!" said O'Neill to Coventry, who made a move to approach the sailor. "My man will do no harm to her Ladyship, and you

THE GRIP OF HONOR

have other matters to attend to, unless you wish to shelter yourself behind a woman's petticoats."

Coventry had been playing for more time, but this was more than he could stand. "I think you have said enough, sir, and if you are ready," he said, "we will talk in another fashion."

"At your service," said the Irishman, composedly. Two swords flashed in the air simultaneously, and rang against each other with deadly purpose a moment after. Both men were masters of the weapon. Coventry had been thoroughly trained in the more direct English school; while O'Neill was a master of all the graceful tricks of the subtle fence of France and Italy. It was as pretty a play — parry and thrust — as one could hope to see, and for a time the advantage was with neither one of them. Elizabeth stood with clasped hands, her face pale with emotion, her lips parted, eagerly watching. The maid as usual was furnishing a comic side to the scene by her screams of "murder — help!" while the sailors were deeply interested in the two combatants.

Finally, after one especially vicious thrust on the part of Coventry, whose foot slipped a little, a clever parry, followed by a dashing *riposte en quarte*, which was met and returned with less skill than usual, O'Neill, with a graceful turn of the wrist, whirled the Englishman's sword from his hand. It flew up into the air and fell clanging on the rocks some distance away.

Coventry was unarmed and helpless before a bitter enemy. He was the stronger of the two, and it

Elizabeth stood with clasped hands, her face pale with emotion, eagerly watching.

SWORDS ARE CROSSED ON THE SAND

flashed into his mind to spring upon his antagonist suddenly, catch him in his arms, and overcome him by brute force; but the glittering point of his enemy's sword, shivering in the sunlight like a serpent's tongue, effectively barred the way. He had played the game and lost. If he must die in the presence of his love, he would do it like a gentleman, on the sword's point.

"Strike, sir!" he said hoarsely, with one quick glance toward Lady Elizabeth, who stood perfectly motionless, looking on in terror. She would have run forward had it not been for old Price.

"Oh, he will be killed, he will be killed!" wailed the maid.

"Sir Englishman, pick up your sword," said O'Neill, lowering his point.

"Sir Irishman," said the other, bowing, "men may call you pirate —"

"Not with impunity, sir," interrupted the touchy O'Neill.

"That I grant you. I was about to add that, whatever they call you, you fight like a gentleman; and it will give me great pleasure to testify to your personal worth at every convenient season. Will you permit me, though I do not know your name, to call you my friend?"

There is a great educational value in the point of a naked sword, and it may account for the sudden change which came over Coventry.

"I shall esteem myself honored, sir. My name is O'Neill, Barry O'Neill, at your service."

THE GRIP OF HONOR

"I shall remember it. You have not only saved the life of Lady Elizabeth Howard, but now you have given me my own."

"Thus am I the prince of match-makers," said O'Neill, bitterly. "I would that I had lost mine in one of the savings!"

"Now, sir," continued Coventry, disregarding this last remark, "if you would be advised by me, withdraw while you may yet do so in safety."

CHAPTER VI

The Master Player takes a Hand

AT this moment, a number of red-coated soldiers clambered down the path in the rocks, while a squad of cavalry came galloping upon the beach by the road at the other end, and, at once dismounting, advanced up the strand. The seamen in the boat, in obedience to a wave of O'Neill's hand, swept her in toward the shore, jumped out, and moved toward him, drawing their cutlasses and handling their pistols threateningly; though they were greatly outnumbered, they would not give up without a struggle. It was Coventry's opportunity now.

"I shall not be able to indulge your desire for the loss of your life," he said, stepping back and picking up his sword, "but I fear that duty imposes upon me the necessity of depriving you of your liberty — I regret the necessity, believe me, 't is a poor return for your generosity, but I have no option."

"What mean you?"

"You are, by your own statements, a rebel against his Majesty. It is my duty as commander of this post and a loyal servant of the king to apprehend you. Indeed, I have been especially charged to look

THE GRIP OF HONOR

out for you. I will promise you and your men the best of treatment, however, and you liberty of action, if you will give me your parole."

"I am twice captured then, it seems," said the lieutenant, looking at Elizabeth, who had come forward as soon as old Price, who had left her, had sprung to his officer's side. As the girl drew near to him, and Major Coventry turned away his head a moment to give an order, the Irishman said to her:

"Why did you not call out to save your lover a moment since?"

"It was not necessary," she said, looking at him with eyes filled with tears. "I knew what you would do." Delay was dangerous to him, — Coventry was posting his men; he hesitated a moment, however, and taking her hand bowed low over it.

"Thank you," he whispered gratefully. "This word, and you, I shall remember."

"And I," said the girl, her eyes filling with tears, "will never forget — "

"Come, sir," said Coventry, dryly, turning at this moment, having finished his dispositions. "I think you overstep the privileges of a parole; and if you will have your men lay down their arms, we will go up to the castle. I have sent for a carriage for you, Elizabeth, which will be here shortly."

"Do you know," said O'Neill, "that I have a mind to say to you that I might as well die right here as at any place else, and I do not think I shall go to that castle, after all. There are seven of us here — "

THE MASTER PLAYER TAKES A HAND

"Close in there!" sharply shouted Coventry to his soldiers, who obeyed him promptly. "Make ready!"

"Handle your pistols, men," cried the other, whipping out his own; but again Elizabeth interfered in the fray. She ran between the American seamen and the English soldiers with outstretched hands.

"Stop!" she cried. "There must be no further fighting here. This gentleman came to this spot to do me a favor, to set me free. My life is his —"

"I give it back to you," cried O'Neill.

"And yours, Major Coventry, was his also," she added reproachfully.

"I give it to him as well; and if any more lives are wanted, anybody can have mine for the taking," interrupted the sailor again.

"This must go no further," continued the girl.

"And it shall not, madam," cried a deep, clear voice, as one of the cutters of the Ranger, filled to the gunwales with heavily armed men, and with a swivel in the bow and a man standing over it with a lighted match in his hand, came sweeping around the headland and dashing in toward the shore. It was under the command of Jones himself, who had grown impatient at the delay.

"I am sorry to interrupt a *tête-à-tête*, gentlemen," he cried.

"You are beaten again, Major Coventry," said O'Neill, calmly. "The odds are in our favor now. Throw down your arms instantly, you dogs," he shouted to the English soldiers. "Back! Out of the way, Miss Howard."

He sprang to her side, and clasping her around the waist as if she had been a child, lifted her out of the line of fire. The jealous Coventry noticed two things, — he did not release her, nor did she struggle to get away. The sullen soldiers rallied about Coventry and presented their arms threateningly; they had no mind either to yield without a fight.

"Stand by!" shouted Jones to the marines in his boat and to the gunners forward.

"Stop, for God's sake stop, Captain Jones! You have been good to me," cried Elizabeth, now struggling faintly to escape from the grasp of O'Neill. "I know that you are a gentleman. That officer is my betrothed. Withhold your fire. They will retire. There must be no blood shed. You promised to set me free and in safety ashore and leave me there. Go, I entreat you!"

"Steady, lads, steady!" cried Jones, stepping out of the boat. "And you, sir," to the English officer, "will you withdraw quietly, taking your lady with you, of course, if we engage to do the same? You are outnumbered, and we can cut you to pieces. Take the word of an older fighter, your honor will be safe, sir."

"You are right, sir, 't is best. I must needs submit, I suppose," said Coventry, resigning himself the more gracefully to the inevitable as he could then receive his love again. "Come, Lady Elizabeth."

THE MASTER PLAYER TAKES A HAND

"Now, why did n't you protest when I was captured?" said O'Neill, releasing her waist, but still holding her hand.

"Could it be because I wanted you to be with me?" she whispered, caught off her guard in spite of herself, with a blush covering her face.

"God bless you for that, and good-bye," he said, bowing over her hand. "A year, give me a year—" he turned and walked away.

"Sir," said Coventry, sheathing his sword, and walking down to where Jones stood upon the sand, "we have been misinformed concerning you. I have had a little interview with your first lieutenant which has convinced me that I was wrong, and this talk has added to my knowledge. As an officer of the king, I offer you my hand. Whatever your political or personal affiliations may be, I am glad to recognize in you gentlemen of merit and distinction. I trust to be able to repay the obligation you have laid upon me and my betrothed on some future occasion. We are friends?"

"Sir," replied Jones, "I love a gallant foe. I shall remember you. I thank you for your courtesy."

"And I as well," added O'Neill.

"It is not the practice of the American Navy," continued Jones, "to force ships of war and bloody battles between loving hearts. Mistress Howard, fare you well; the Ranger, her officers and crew, are yours if you wish. If we should be met by another ship with you in command, we strike to you without a blow."

THE GRIP OF HONOR

"Elizabeth," said Coventry, magnanimously, "can you not bid your friends good-bye?"

"I shall ever remember Captain John Paul Jones," said Lady Elizabeth, stepping forward and giving the little captain her hand to kiss, "and I shall never forget Lieutenant O'Neill."

"Will you wait one year for him?" he whispered as he bowed low over her hand.

"Come and see," she answered, and turned away.

BOOK II
THEY MEET AGAIN

CHAPTER VII

After a Long Time

"THERE are only two men-of-war in the whole lot."

"Right, yer Honor. That 'un near the shore there-away looks like a big frigate. That 'll be the Serapis, I'm thinkin'."

"Yes, and that one further out, the Scarborough."

"Ay, ay, sir, an' all the rest on 'em is merchantmen. There ain't a gun on board any on 'em. Nice pickin's them 'll be fer us poor sailormen arter we dispose of them war-vessels. Dash my wig! jist think of them fat traders, an' we a-rummagin' among 'em — "

"That will do, Price. Just moderate your transports a little," said the officer, stepping forward to the brow of the hill and taking another long look at the harbor.

"I ain't no transport," muttered the garrulous old man under his breath. "I won't carry no soldiers nowhere. I'm a man-o'-war, I am;" but he took good care that his superior should not hear these somewhat insubordinate remarks.

"Well," said the other, finally turning about after his close scrutiny, "I think we have ascertained about all we have come for. They are the Baltic convoy, without doubt, and you would better make a straight course for the ship at once and report."

"An' you, sir?" asked the old man, respectfully, "won't you come along, sir? I hate to cut cable an' leave you here adrift, alone, yer Honor."

"No," answered the officer, after a reflective pause, "I think I shall go up to that castle on the bluff beyond and find out a little more definitely as to the situation, if possible. Meanwhile, do you get on your horse and ride back to Bridlington Bay. Go aboard the Alert and tell Mr. Lunt, from me, to join the Richard to the southward at once, and notify Captain Jones of what we have seen. Tell him I think it will be perfectly safe for him to come on: there is a great fleet of merchant ships here with only two ships-of-war; he will rejoice at the chance of a fair fight. I will find means to join him at the rendezvous before the rest of the ships can assemble and they can get under way. Now bear a hand; don't let the grass grow under your keel."

"Oh, Lord, yer Honor, have I got to git on board that 'ere four-legged craft agin?" said old Price, ruefully.

"That's what you have to do, my lad," remarked the officer, cheerfully.

"Seems like somethin's wrong with him," said the old sailor. "A animal wot steers by the head is contrary like to natur. Now if I could only git him to go about on t'other tack, or wear him, by shiftin' his tail, I'd understand him perfectly; but this yere tiller rope riggin' over his bows is wot gits me. An', sir, I can't make out with them 'ere stirrups nuther; it's like hangin' onto the yard-arm in a tossin' sea without no foot ropes. Howsomever, if I must, I must, I guess."

"Oh, you won't mind it," replied the officer, laughing at the old man's rueful face. "Besides, the wind's fair, and you'll be going free most of the way. Just give him a touch of your weather heel once in a while, and you'll soon make the harbor."

"I never thought about the wind," said the veteran gunner, thoughtfully, his face brightening as he turned and listened for it. "Yer Honor's right. 'T will be plain sailin'. Well, sir, anchor's aweigh, an' here goes!"

The old seaman, giving great evidence of his disinclination in spite of the favoring breeze, at last climbed upon the back of his staid old horse, and, resisting the temptation to give him his direction by a pull of the tail, got under way and lurched rapidly down the road. Left to himself, the lieutenant mounted his own horse — surprising to state, for a sailor he was an excellent horseman — and rode down toward the sleeping town nestled around Scarborough harbor, which was filled with a large fleet of merchant ships convoyed by two men-of-war, all riding quietly at their anchors.

Opposite the acclivity on which the two men had stood, and to the north of the town, rose a bold, splendid headland, or scar, almost an island, to the height of about three hundred feet. The rugged crest was crowned by a picturesque old castle. The headland jutted boldly out into the sea, and the wild waters dashed upon its walls from every side. Access to the castle from the town was by means of a causeway and bridge springing over a rocky and otherwise impassable connection between the cliff and the mainland, which was sometimes flooded at high-tide.

Portions of the castle were in bad repair, or had been dismantled in the several wars in which it had played a memorable part since its erection nearly seven hundred years before by a follower of William the Conqueror; but a large part of it was still inhabitable, and had been provided with a sufficient garrison. A heavy water battery, which had been placed in position during the rebellion in 1745, had been recently strengthened and reinforced.

Captain Jones, in the Bon Homme Richard, had been cruising around the coasts of the British Islands for some time. He had heard of the expected arrival of the Baltic fleet in these waters, and had presumed that they would make Scarborough harbor. Word had been received from a small trader he had overhauled, that a large number of ships had assembled in that harbor; and in order to ascertain whether he might safely attack them with his small nondescript squadron, he had accepted the voluntary services of Lieutenant O'Neill, seconded by gunner Price of the Bon Homme Richard.

They had gone on ahead of the squadron in the cutter Alert, and had landed below Scarborough

AFTER A LONG TIME

headland, and ridden on to Scarborough to ascertain the facts. The Alert was to carry the news back to Jones, on the Richard, farther down the coast, and the vessels of his squadron were all to assemble a day or two later at Bridlington Bay, a small and unimportant town with a good harbor within easy reaching distance of the expected prey. Should the report of the scouts be favorable, they would proceed at once to attack the convoy.

On their journey to Scarborough, O'Neill had ascertained from a passing countryman that Lord Westbrooke was still governor of the castle, and he at once surmised that Lady Elizabeth Howard would probably be there with her guardian. Six months more than the year he had asked for from her had elapsed, and many untoward circumstances had prevented him from carrying out his plan of seeking her, but she had ever been in his heart, and time and separation had but intensified his passion. The mercurial Irishman had been deeply smitten by the proud English beauty, and the constancy of his devotion evidenced the depth of the impression she had made upon him.

When Jones had returned with the Ranger from his first successful cruise, he and his officers had been fêted and made much of by the French court. The gallant adventures in which he had participated lent a new charm to the fascinating personality of the son of the old marshal, whose entrée was already everything that could be desired; and his heart, accordingly, had been a target for repeated attacks

THE GRIP OF HONOR

upon the part of the bright-eyed and fascinating dames of France — but to no avail had they attempted its capture.

Something of the story of his devotion had been allowed to leak out, however, to account for his obduracy, and they finally understood why he was so unusually insensible to their charms. This romance naturally only added a piquancy to the feminine pursuit of which he was the object, although the ladies' sportive love chase proved, in the end, unavailing. He had resolved, O'Neill said, to show the world that unusual spectacle, a constant Irishman! This was to attempt the impossible, had been the quick reply, but, nevertheless, he had accomplished it.

Our Celtic mariner did not resign from the American service, however, not because he cared particularly for America, for democratic doctrines could never be acceptable to a follower of the young Stuart, the intimate associate of the young nobles of France; but, primarily, because he saw in it renewed opportunities to annoy and humiliate the stout Hanoverian whom he and his people hated, and from whom they had received much harm, and, secondly, because he was so much attracted by the strong personality of Paul Jones. So great had become his regard for this wonderful man that he had even waived considerations of rank in favor of an American, the gallant Richard Dale, and had consented to serve as second lieutenant instead of first, on the Richard, when that famous ship and her

AFTER A LONG TIME

ill-assorted consorts started forth upon the memorable cruise.

The tacticians of the French Navy unfortunately were not given to consider downright hard fighting as the end and aim of naval enterprise. Their manœuvres were calculated to annoy and harass the enemy, but their first thought was not to destroy his ships, but to protect their own, — a fatal mistake in policy from which they have ever suffered.

This was not John Paul Jones' way. Whatever else he was, he was a fighter from the beginning to the end, and O'Neill found in him a congenial spirit. The love-lorn Irishman had tried several times to communicate with Lady Elizabeth by letter and messenger, but without success, for he received no reply to his letters, and his messengers had never returned. Therefore, when he found himself in such close proximity to her as on this, the evening of Tuesday, the 21st of September, 1779, he was utterly unable to resist the temptation at least to attempt to see her again.

Jones and the ships were not due at the rendezvous until the day after the next day, that would be Thursday morning. There would be ample time to rejoin them on the next day, Wednesday. O'Neill imagined himself perfectly safe; he had used no disguise except to wear the uniform of a French naval officer, and as France and England were nominally at peace, he persuaded himself that he was in no danger. It was a breach of military propriety, he admitted, of course, but nothing more, — this failure to return promptly to his ship, — and for that he was willing to suffer.

With the delightful casuistry of lovers he persuaded himself against his better judgment and failed to see his action in its true military significance. Trusting to audacity, mother wit, and Dan Cupid for protection, he went bravely on. In fact, he was taking his life in his hand. His love blinded him, — it is the chief function of the cherubic god; without that power most matches he attempts would fail. Meanwhile, with a beating heart — beating not from fear, but with anticipation — he rode slowly down the hill and into the town, where he left his horse at an inn, and made his way on foot, and supperless, such his eagerness, toward the castle.

He had no definite plan. There did not seem to be room for any. He had one consuming desire: to see, to speak to, to come in touch again with the beautiful girl who had been the object of his every thought, the end of his every desire, the spirit of every dream in which he had indulged since they had met. He had a thought — a hope — that she was still Elizabeth Howard. There was that in her promise, in her look, in her word, when she had said, "Come and see" on the strand, which gave him the hope that she would wait until he did come, be it one year or two; and with the sanguine spirit of his race he could not prepare himself for a disappointment.

The moon had risen as he walked quietly through the town and began to mount the hill. He did not know how to gain admittance to the castle when he

AFTER A LONG TIME

approached it; and as ill luck would have it, as he was standing on the causeway looking toward the gate, he was approached by a squad of soldiers under the command of a sergeant, who were returning from an errand in the town. His meditations, as he stood gazing at the lights shining from the different windows, wondering behind which wall was ensconced the idol of his heart, were rudely interrupted by the grasp of a rough hand upon his shoulder and a harsh voice in his ear saying, —

"Well, sir, wot are you a-doin' 'ere at this hour o' the night? Entrance to the castle is forbid to every one except members of the garrison, or them wich has passes. No one is allowed on the causeway after sunset even. There's so many tales of raidin's an' hell's own doin's on the coast by that bloody ravagin' pirate Jones an' his bleedin' gang, that we're a'most in a state of siege. Give an account of yourself."

"My friend," said O'Neill, calmly, glancing rapidly about him, and giving up at once any idea of resistance, for he was surrounded by at least a dozen men, one or two of whom had laid violent hands upon him, — "my friend," he said, speaking in broken English, with a well-simulated French accent, "I am an officer of the King of France, travelling for pleasure through your great country. I hear of the old castle — I wish to see it — hence I come here. I have done nothing — you will let me go free?"

"A Frenchman?"

"Yes, monsieur, I have that honor."

THE GRIP OF HONOR

"Well, that settles it. You've got to come along with us now. A frog-eatin' Frenchman's our natural-born enemy."

"But, monsieur, there is no war between my master and your king?"

"Don't monshur me. I don't take no palaverin', an' I don't know nothin' about whether there is war or not," said the sergeant, brusquely; "but we always did hate the bloody Frenchies, an' we always will, an' whenever we ketch one of 'em around here, he's got to give an account of hisself. Now if you come along peaceable like, all right — we won't hurt you. If you don't, we'll just pick you up and carry you. You can take your choice," he added indifferently.

A horseman galloping in from the town at this moment drew rein in front of the little group.

"Ah, sergeant, what is it? Whom have you there?" he queried sharply.

"'T is a Frenchman, sir. We found him a-prowlin' round here. He's a spy, I takes it," answered the sergeant, saluting but still retaining his grasp.

"Pardon me, monsieur," said O'Neill; "I am no spy. I am a gentleman of France, as I explain to this man. I travel — come here to see the castle —"

"Well, sir, I can assist you to attain your end," interrupted the lieutenant on the horse; "and since you desire to see the castle, perhaps you would not object to taking a look at it from the inside."

"As a prisoner, monsieur?"

"Well, I am sorry you put it that way, but I shall be compelled to turn you over to the governor."

AFTER A LONG TIME

"But I protest, monsieur!"

"You can protest to the admiral if you wish, the governor, I mean, for you will have to come along now, under the circumstances. We hear that d——d Scots buccaneer Paul Jones is on the coast, and we don't know when he might strike or whom he might send on shore. We can't be too careful, you know."

"Very well, monsieur, I come," said O'Neill, shrugging his shoulders and resigning himself gracefully to the inevitable.

"That's good," answered the young officer. "Bring him along, sergeant."

"Yes, leftenant. Now, you Johnnie, right about face, march!"

It was in this unexpected and undignified manner that O'Neill gained entrance to the castle. As they walked beneath the great gates of the gloomy fortress, his heart, in spite of the serious nature of his position, gave a bound of elation. This reckless young man had as yet no other thought than that by every step he had been brought a little nearer to his divinity; if other thoughts had come, it is doubtful if he would have allowed them to stop him now. As the party halted in the courtyard, while the lieutenant dismounted and hastened to apprise the governor of the capture, he even ventured most imprudently to ask the sergeant if Lady Elizabeth Howard was in the castle.

"She is," replied the astonished functionary. "Wot's that to you, I'd like to know?"

CHAPTER VIII

Lady Elizabeth does not know the Marquis de Richemont

BEFORE he could answer, an order came for the prisoner to be brought forward. After ascending a flight of worn stone steps and going through a long dark passage, a great door was thrown open at its end, and he was confronted by a blaze of light which dazzled him at first, until, his eyes becoming accustomed to the illumination, he realized that he stood on the threshold of a splendid hall in the old keep, which had possibly once been the banqueting hall of the castle. Long lancet windows upon one side, their leaded frames filled with rich painted glass, looked out upon the sea, whose waves beating ceaselessly upon the bluff below filled the room with a subdued murmur like a strain of hushed and vibrant music, such was the elevation of the tower.

The room was massively and splendidly furnished with heavy antique furniture. The stone walls were covered with hangings of rich old tapestry from the famous looms of Arras. Here and there were portraits of distinguished members of the Westbrooke family, — women renowned for their lustrous beauty, or men who, holding the castle at different times, had made their names famous by their bravery and

MARQUIS DE RICHEMONT

skill. The prisoner's feet sank into a thick, soft, luxurious carpet stretched upon the stone flags of the old floor.

Writing at a large table standing near the centre of the room and covered with candelabra, sat a bewigged old man of commanding presence dressed in a naval uniform covered with orders and stars bespeaking high rank. Farther away, with her back turned to the light, and to the door by which he had entered, a young woman sat, apparently reading intently. One glance at the graceful curve of her neck and the exquisite poise of her head told him it was she. Forgetful of everything else, he would have stepped forward, had it not been for the restraining hand of the sergeant.

"The prisoner, m' Lud," said the latter, saluting.

The admiral continued his writing a moment, and then looking up fixed his eyes keenly upon the young man. His first glance told him that he had to deal with no ordinary prisoner. He rose at once and bowed with the courtesy of a finished gentleman.

"Have the goodness to step forward, sir, and be seated," he said, pointing to the chair. "Sergeant, remain on guard where you are."

With an equally low bow to the older man, O'Neill took a few steps in his direction and sat down on the indicated chair in front of the admiral, facing him and the woman beyond, who, still intent upon her book or lost in thought, had not yet noticed his entrance. Prisoners, in fact, being every-day occurrences at the castle in these troublous times, they

THE GRIP OF HONOR

had ceased to interest her; still the unusual complaisance of the old man, as expressed by his voice and manner, attracted her attention; she looked up from the book without turning her head, and listened.

"I am sorry to subject you to any annoyance, sir," continued the admiral, "but the rules are very strict, and I must abide by my own regulations. We apprehend a descent upon our coast by the notorious pirate, John Paul Jones—" O'Neill started violently and bit his lip, but said nothing—"and it is my duty to take unusual precautions," added the speaker. "I must ask your name, your station, and business here."

"I am the—" said O'Neill, quietly, but with his glance fixed on the powdered head showing over the chair-back opposite him.

There was a commotion at the other side of the table. Lady Elizabeth sprang to her feet with a hurried exclamation, dropped her book to the floor, and then turned quickly, and stepped toward the other two. O'Neill and the admiral both rose at the same time.

She was *en grande tenue,* her hair rolled high and powdered, jewels sparkling about the snowy throat, which rose from the pale blue silk of her corsage.

"It is—" she cried.

"The Marquis de Richemont, at your service, mademoiselle," O'Neill interrupted quickly, bowing low before her, fearing lest in her surprise she would betray him.

"Good heavens, Elizabeth! what is the meaning of

this? Do you know this man?" asked the admiral, in great astonishment.

"Every traveller," smilingly interrupted O'Neill, suavely, striving to give Elizabeth time to collect herself, with the appearance of the greatest *sang-froid* himself, though his heart was beating so rapidly he could scarce maintain his composure, "on these islands has heard of the beauty of Lady Elizabeth Howard. Her reputation as a woman of charm has even extended to the continent whence I come. It was in the hope of having the privilege of seeing her that I walked up toward the castle this evening. I have not the honor of her acquaintance, monsieur."

"Do you know this man, Elizabeth?" persisted the admiral, sternly, his suspicions aroused by her actions.

There was evidently some mystery about his coming, and the girl was quick to see that to proclaim O'Neill's name and occupation would probably place him in an embarrassing position, to say the least. She recovered herself by a great effort, and turning away languidly, remarked with well-assumed carelessness, —

"I? Certainly not, sir. I have never heard of the Marquis de Richemont before in my life." The statement was absolutely correct, the Irishman's rank having been kept strictly in abeyance. O'Neill shrugged his shoulders and extended his hands in confirmation of her words.

"Why that cry, then, and your surprise, madam?" questioned the still unconvinced admiral.

THE GRIP OF HONOR

"I know not, sir; I must have been dreaming, and the sound of a strange voice startled me."

"Beg pardon, m' Lud," said the sergeant, saluting; "yer Worship, he axed if Lady Elizabeth Howard lived 'ere, wen he was down in the courtyard."

"Silence, sirrah!" thundered the old admiral, who allowed no one to entertain doubts of his ward but himself. "Do you mean to imply that Lady Elizabeth has knowledge of this gentleman?"

"Oh, sergeant!" said the girl, clasping her hands and looking at the old veteran with all the fascination of which she was capable.

"No, yer Ludship, no, sir. O' course not; certainly not, yer Honor," returned the man, in great confusion. "I spoke by way o' showin' that's wot he come for."

"It was in pursuance of my desire to see so great a beauty that I asked the question, monsieur."

"Sir, your admiration does me too much honor," said Elizabeth, courtesying.

"I make up for the fact that your reputation does your Ladyship too little, then, mademoiselle," he answered.

"Enough of this," said the admiral, impatiently. "The girl is well enough; but you did n't come here to look at her, did you?"

"On my honor as a gentleman, monsieur, for no other purpose."

"Well, give some account of yourself otherwise, and perhaps if it be satisfactory, as you have accomplished that purpose, I may send you on your way rejoicing," said the admiral, amused at the extravagance of the young man.

"No man could leave the presence of Lady Elizabeth Howard rejoicing, sir."

"Damnation, sir!" cried the governor, testily, "are you going to stand here and bandy compliments about all day like a French dancing-master?"

"I have nothing further to urge for my words, my Lord, when my excuse stands in your very presence."

The governor looked at the two young people in great perplexity.

"I fear, my dear Marquis de Richemont," said he ironically, "unless you can give some more coherent account of yourself, I shall be under the painful necessity of having you locked up, in which case the only divinity you will be allowed to gaze upon will be the lovely face and figure of yonder sergeant."

"Yes, yer Ludship, I —" remarked the sergeant, grimacing.

"Silence, sirrah!" thundered the admiral.

"My Lord," answered O'Neill, smiling, "it is very simple. I am an officer in the navy of the King of France, making a tour of England for pleasure. I came here to this town this evening. I hear of the great admiral, Lord Westbrooke, in his great castle, and the beauty of his ward, Lady Elizabeth Howard. I am a lover of the beautiful. I stand on the causeway gazing at the castle. Your soldiers arrest me and bring me here. I rejoice to find Lady Elizabeth more beautiful than I have dreamed. A year and a half have only intensified her charms."

"A year and a half! Dreams, sir! What mean you by that, pray? What have the years to do with the matter? Did you see her a year and a half since?" cried the admiral, suspiciously again.

O'Neill started; it was a fatal slip, but he hastened to repair it as best he could.

"I have seen her picture, sir."

"And where, pray, have you seen her picture?"

"In the possession of an English officer, a friend of mine whom I met at Liverpool a year and a half ago," answered O'Neill, audaciously.

"And who was this English officer, pray, who displayed my picture?" interrupted Elizabeth, with an appearance of great agitation.

"Major Edward Coventry, mademoiselle."

"Oh, Edward! Why, God bless me," said the admiral, genially, "he is my son. Do you mean to tell me you are a friend of his? Why did n't you say so before?"

"I had the honor of his acquaintance," said O'Neill, bowing gravely, "on one very interesting and memorable occasion indeed, when he was on duty at the Château Birkenhead, I believe."

"Yes, that would be about a year and a half ago. Sir, in that case you are very welcome to this castle," said the admiral, "and now I beg leave to present you in due and proper form to my ward. Lady Elizabeth Howard, permit me to introduce to you the Marquis de Richemont."

"I am charmed to have the pleasure of meeting

the marquis," responded the girl, smiling and courtesying deeply.

"The pleasure and the honor are mine, mademoiselle," responded O'Neill, fully entering upon the comedy of the moment.

"And," continued the admiral, "as my son, Major Edward Coventry, has sent me word he will be here shortly, you can renew your acquaintance with him."

It was as if he had exploded a bomb-shell in the room.

"Edward! Coming here?" cried Elizabeth, her voice filled with terror at the unfortunate event, which she vainly endeavored to conceal. "What for? Why did you not tell me?"

"He desired to surprise you, my dear," answered the admiral, wondering again at her agitation; "you know your wedding takes place next week."

"Ah, a wedding!" said O'Neill, starting and looking at Elizabeth. "Mademoiselle is then to marry?"

"Yes, your friend Major Coventry," replied the old man, — "an old engagement."

"I refused to marry him for a year, and for six months more. I waited all that time. There was no word," she said slowly to O'Neill, as if each word were wrung from her by his intent look, her pale cheeks flooded with color.

"Have you taken leave of your senses, Elizabeth?" continued the admiral, in great surprise; "of what interest to a stranger is your — er — maidenly hesitation?"

"Anything which concerns so fair a lady is of deep interest to your humble servant," answered O'Neill, ironically and bitterly. The comedy had gone, tragedy, as ever, following hard upon it.

A door at the rear of the room was opened softly at this moment; and a young man in the brilliant scarlet uniform of a British officer, entered and stepped lightly toward them. His glance fell first upon the speaker.

"Barry O'Neill, by heaven!" he exclaimed, springing eagerly forward with outstretched hand. "How came you here?" For a moment the young soldier was oblivious of the presence of his father and his betrothed. His untimely entrance filled the room with apprehension and dismay.

CHAPTER IX

The Picture on the Wall

"O'NEILL?" said the admiral, in much bewilderment; "Edward, this is your friend, the Marquis de Richemont."

"Edward, do not speak!" cried Lady Elizabeth, distractedly.

"Ah, Elizabeth, my love and duty to you, but not speak? About what, pray? What mean you?"

"Is this gentleman, the Marquis de Richemont, your friend or not, sir? Cease this by-play, Elizabeth; I will have an explanation," demanded the now thoroughly aroused admiral.

"My friend? Quite so," said Major Coventry, smiling. "Though I was ignorant that he was a marquis, he is none the less welcome. I am exceedingly glad to see him again. You too, I presume, Elizabeth?"

"Glad even as you are," she replied deliberately, now seeing that further concealment was useless.

"But you called him O'Neill," continued the admiral.

"That is my name, sir," said O'Neill, calmly, recognizing the uselessness of further evasion. "I am one of the Irish O'Neills, formerly of County Clare, now in the service of the King of France." He could not have said it more proudly had he been the king himself.

"The last time I saw you, you were on the Ranger, that American Continental ship," continued Coventry.

"As a prisoner, sir?" cried the admiral.

"As an officer, my Lord," answered the Irishman.

"What, sir! And now you are —"

"Second lieutenant of the American Continental ship Bon Homme Richard, Captain John Paul Jones, at your service," was the dauntless reply.

"Good gad!" said the admiral, "is it possible? And you, Elizabeth, you have deceived me also. You knew this man?"

"Yes, sir, but not as the Marquis de Richemont."

"You have met this gentleman before?"

"Yes, sir."

"Where, may I ask, and when?"

"About a year and a half since, sir. You remember when the Maidstone was wrecked? He saved me from death then, and after Captain Jones put me ashore, you know —"

"He spared my life too, as well, sir, at that time," said Coventry; "they both did."

"You seem to be a good hand at saving lives, Lieutenant O'Neill, Marquis de Richemont, perhaps you can think now of some way of saving your own," remarked the admiral, sarcastically.

"'T is useless to me now, my Lord, and not worth the saving," answered the young man, calmly; "but I would not have you mar the approaching nuptials of your son and ward by an execution. Let me at

THE PICTURE ON THE WALL

least live until after the wedding. I shall be more willing to die then," he added softly.

"You came here for what purpose?" continued the admiral, disregarding the latter words of the young man as utterly irrelevant.

"To find out the number and force and disposition of the ships in the harbor."

"At the instance of—"

"Captain Jones, sir."

"The murdering pirate!"

"I have resented such language and proved its falsity upon the person of your son, sir," burst out O'Neill, stepping forward, his hand upon his sword. "Shall I impose the same lesson on the father?"

"You are a prisoner, sir," replied the admiral, imperturbably, "and are here at my pleasure to receive, not to give lessons. Stand back, sir! Sergeant, bring in a file of men for a guard. Deliver up your sword at once, sir, to Major Coventry!"

"Your Lordship is master here; I obey," answered the Irishman, shrugging his shoulders, and drawing his sword, he tendered it to Major Coventry, who stepped forward reluctantly to receive it.

"Father," he said respectfully, "so far as my knowledge goes, Captain Jones is certainly a gentleman. Had it not been for his magnanimity and that of my friend — I may still call you that, sir?"

"I am vastly honored, sir, I am sure."

"— my friend, the Marquis de Richemont, you would be childless to-day. Had it not been for the courage of this gentleman, Lady Elizabeth here —"

THE GRIP OF HONOR

"Oh, sir!" cried Elizabeth, impetuously, "they are men of honor. I pray you release this officer and let him go free. Nay, never shake your head; I ask it as a wedding gift to me, sir."

"My liberty your wedding gift, mademoiselle? Never!" interrupted O'Neill, firmly.

"Say no more, either of you," said the admiral, decisively. "You, sir, came here as an enemy, a spy."

"Not so, sir. I came here in the uniform of a French officer."

"But that is not the uniform of the flag under which you now serve," continued the admiral, keenly. "You may secure some consideration, however, at my hands as representing his Majesty the King, God bless him! by revealing the circumstances and plans and the ultimate purpose of your rebellious captain."

"Clearly an impossible proposition," said O'Neill, bowing.

"But stop!" said the admiral, "now that I recall it, you gave me your word of honor that you came here to see this lady."

"And that is true, sir. I might have escaped to my ship with ease, in possession of the information I desired to get, but I came up to the castle to see her."

"A most foolish excursion, sir, and why, pray?"

"Because I love her," said O'Neill, calmly.

"What!" cried Coventry, in great surprise and dismay. "Did you know this, Elizabeth?"

"Is a woman ever ignorant of the feelings she

THE PICTURE ON THE WALL

excites in a lover's breast, sir?" O'Neill answered for her.

"And have you — did you — " continued Coventry, looking still at Elizabeth.

"Lady Elizabeth has done nothing, sir. No word of affection has ever crossed her lips, to me at least," again replied O'Neill. "She would not even wait."

"Oh, but she did," interrupted Coventry, jealously, "a year — six months — she tried to postpone her wedding for six months more. I begin to understand."

"Peace, Edward!" said Elizabeth, trembling violently; "the Marquis de Richemont is — is nothing to me — can never be anything to me, that is. The wedding shall proceed at the appointed date; I gave you my word. It was the wish of my mother, the wish of the admiral, your wish — "

"And yours, also, dearest Elizabeth, is it not?" said Coventry, taking her hand entreatingly. She hesitated and stood silent.

"Have me executed at once, sir, in mercy and pity," said O'Neill to the admiral; "let it be now — the sooner the better. This I cannot stand; 't is too much."

"Not so," replied the admiral, gravely; "I will consider the matter further and consult with you again. Meanwhile, if you will give me your parole, I will allow you the freedom of the castle."

"Parole! 'T is given, sir. Faith, I hardly think you could drive me away."

"That's well," returned the admiral. "Sergeant,

call my steward and have him assign chambers to the Marquis de Richemont. Coventry, I presume you will place your wardrobe at his disposal in case he needs anything. Now the marquis will doubtless wish to retire. We will see him in the morning. Come, Elizabeth. Good-night, sir; the sergeant will attend you."

"Lord Westbrooke, I thank you. Major Coventry, your servant. Lady Elizabeth, I wish you joy on your wedding; good-night," replied the young man, bowing to them all in succession.

As the admiral and the others left the room, the young lieutenant sank down on his chair and put his head upon his hands upon the table. The old sergeant, who had seen it all, watched him a moment in silence. Walking up to him finally, and laying his hand on his shoulder with the familiarity of a privileged character, he said, —

"Come now, sir, be a soldier."

"You can give no worse advice than that to a sailor, my friend," replied O'Neill, rising and smiling in spite of his misery. "Lead on, I will follow," he added.

As they passed down the great hall, the eyes of the wretched lieutenant fell upon a large picture hanging rather low on the wall in a far corner above a dais near the doorway. It was the portrait of a beautiful woman in the fashion of some fifty years back. She was seated in a great carved oak chair, the counterpart of and evidently painted from one sitting beneath it. In face and feature the portrait

THE PICTURE ON THE WALL

was a striking likeness of Lady Elizabeth Howard. The skill of the painter had been so great, the colors had been so nicely chosen, so delicately laid on, that in the flickering, uncertain candle-light, which left this part of the room in a rather deep shadow, the picture actually seemed to breathe. O'Neill stopped as if petrified.

"Come along, sir," said the sergeant, gruffly.

"A moment, if you please, my friend — a moment. What sort of a man are you to pass by such as this without notice? It should be Lady Elizabeth, but the fashion of the dress — "

"It's her mother, sir, a cousin of the admiral's. I pass it every day, sir, an' I've got so I don't take no notice on it, no more. She was a young thing, scarce older than her young Leddyship when she set for that paintin', an' they had no children for years, leastaways they all died till this baby was born, an' then she died too. I've been attached to the admiral's service in one way or another sence I was a boy, an' dandled her many a time on my knee. Yes, and her young Leddyship, Lady Elizabeth that is, too, wen she was a little girl."

"My regard for you goes up a thousand-fold, my friend," said O'Neill, smiling; "I could almost envy you your opportunities. Would I had been you!"

"'T ain't no use wishin' that," said the old sergeant, shaking his head; "there never was no Frenchman could ever take my place."

"Quite right," replied O'Neill, smiling; "'t would be clearly impossible."

THE GRIP OF HONOR

"Come along, then, yer Honor."

"Stay a moment," returned the enraptured Irishman; "a year at gaze would not sate me with the beauty of this picture. How like is the fair image!" murmured the entranced young man, approaching nearer and fairly holding his breath under the influence of the moment. He stretched out his hand toward the painting with a little reverential gesture.

"Look out, sir!" said the sergeant, warningly; "the picture hangs very loose, an' the frame — "

What evil fate was it that determined its fall at that moment? There was a tremendous crash, something gave way, and the great frame dropped from its place on the wall and fell across the heavy oaken chair which stood beneath it, and the picture was impaled upon its Gothic points. The two men sprang to seize it and lift it up. Alas! it had been literally torn to pieces. The canvas had evidently been originally a defective one, for it had split in every direction. Restoration was clearly impossible.

"Good Heaven!" said the Irishman, "what a misfortune!"

"It had to come, an' it's too late to be mended now," said the sergeant, philosophically, "so we must get on."

"Very good," said O'Neill, tenderly lifting the frame, with the rags of the tattered canvas hanging to it, back against the wall; "there is nothing to keep us here now. Unlucky fool that I am, even the semblance of the original is not for me!"

CHAPTER X

Lady Elizabeth will keep her Word

THE night fell on three of the most unhappy people in the world; yet to each had been vouchsafed a partial realization of a cherished hope. Coventry should have been luxuriating in the thought of his approaching marriage to the girl he loved; Elizabeth should have been overwhelmed with joy at the reappearance of O'Neill, after his long absence; and O'Neill during that time had asked for nothing but an opportunity to stand once more in the presence of his divinity. The desire of each had been granted, and yet all three were completely miserable.

Coventry, because he more than suspected that Elizabeth loved O'Neill; Elizabeth, because she felt that honor compelled her to marry Coventry, to whom she was deeply attached, but toward whom her feelings, she now found, were vastly different from those which had flooded her being with new life at the sight of the young Irishman. Her period of waiting and dreaming had unconsciously developed a passion for him which had broken all barriers at the mere sound of his voice, the sight of his face. As for O'Neill, he found her fairer than he had ever thought even in his most extravagant dreams, and it was in an agony of despair that he contemplated her as the bride of another. There was this saving grace in his position, however: he would probably be condemned to death forthwith, and he was in no mood to balk the executioner; if ever death be welcome, it would be so to him.

The only one who was completely at his ease, and who, in fact, extracted a certain satisfaction from the situation, was the admiral. Naturally he did not enter very deeply into the matrimonial schemes of the young, and with the indifference of the aged and the present, he doubted that it would be a matter of any great difficulty either to make Elizabeth forget, if necessary, the Irishman in whom even his obtuse vision had detected that she was greatly interested; or, in case it suited his purpose better, to make his son forget Elizabeth in the presence of some other charmer whom he might select. His purpose was, as ever, the paramount consideration with the admiral.

He had conceived a brilliant idea, which he fondly hoped would result, were it to be realized, in the capture of the notorious Paul Jones, who was the object of consuming desire on the part of every military and naval man in the three kingdoms. So enchanted was the old man with his own idea, and so desirous was he of bagging the game, that he would not have hesitated to sacrifice the affections of his son, the happiness of his ward, or to brush aside almost anything, save his honor, which might stand in his way.

LADY ELIZABETH

The young Irishman had clearly forfeited his life by his action; nay, more, now that he recalled his name he remembered that he had been found guilty of high treason, and, like his father, was under sentence of death for that as well; he had a double hold upon him, therefore. The powers of the admiral, who was one of the leading men of the realm, were unusually large, and as a state of martial law had been proclaimed on the coast, he was supreme as to life and death, in matters where any military exigency could be urged.

He chuckled to himself at the thought that he held in his hand two of the master cards, — love of life and love of woman; the third, love of honor, which O'Neill was possessed of, was a high one, to be sure, but he trusted by clever play to win the game, since the odds were with him. Elizabeth had become a State paper — a pledge in pawn — to him; O'Neill another piece, or player. He had not yet formulated any plan for carrying out his great idea, but one was already germinating in his mind, so that in the end, under the stimulus of the splendid opportunity he saw before him for rounding out an already brilliant career in the service of his country, by effecting the capture of the famous Paul Jones, his hours were as sleepless as were those of the others.

The poor Irish lieutenant had caused a great deal of trouble to every one with whom he had come in contact. Even Paul Jones himself, who loved and cherished the young man with all his generous heart, was filled with deep anxiety as to his probable fate, when he heard the report of old Price the next day, especially as the hours fled away and his lieutenant did not rejoin the ship. In spite of the absence of the rest of his squadron, the commodore at once hastened to the rendezvous with the Richard alone, and there determined to take a small hand in the game himself while waiting for the Pallas, the Alliance, and the others to assemble. Cautious inquiries which he caused to be made on shore had informed him that, as he expected, O'Neill had been apprehended. A less kindly man than Paul Jones would have left him to his fate — but that was not his way.

Early the next morning, being Wednesday, September the twenty-second, O'Neill had arisen and gone down on the terrace of the castle overlooking the ocean and the ships in the harbor, where he met Lady Elizabeth. She was gazing listlessly over the causeway at a horseman galloping along the road.

"Do I interrupt reminiscences of a *tête-à-tête*, madam?" said he, saluting her with a profound bow.

"Reminiscences such as mine are better interrupted," she replied.

"You were —."

"Saying good-bye to my — my — cousin."

"Has your ladyship no dearer title than that by which to designate him?"

"Not yet," she answered wearily.

"Ah, I perceive," he continued jealously, "the

natural regret at the absence of your betrothed, for — "

"No, no, not that! How can you trifle so with me at this moment? He reproached me because I — why do I tell you these things? You constrain me, sir; I — "

"Forgive me; you need not finish, Lady Elizabeth," he said with a sudden gravity. "As for me, I must needs trifle, or die. Life in the freshness of the morning, the white-capped ocean stretching before us in the sunlight, the gentle breeze playing across our faces, is sweet to think on; with youth and rank and station, it would be heavenly spent with you. Without you I welcome the death your guardian will undoubtedly inflict upon me."

"Yet you waited so long — a year and a half — why did you not come? I — " She stopped. She had spoken in a low, tender whisper, looking down at the sea beneath them, and plucking nervously at the loose plaster of the old walk. Death so imminent for love and lover — nay, not for love; that were eternal — broke down petty convention. Where were death and love, there, too, should truth and honesty be — and honor.

He laid his strong hand gently down on the small white one outlined upon the gray weather-beaten rock of the parapet; with upturned palm she met his grasp. Her eyes were lifted now; she drew strength from his strength; a dawning hope flickered into being in her torn heart. He was so strong and true, he surely could do something — there must be some other way. It was the tribute woman pays to man.

He read aright, with eyes keen from affection, the mute, piteous appeal in her sweetly lifted face. But he could only smile sadly in answer, with a silent shake of the head. There was no other way, then, in the marked path she must walk. Have mercy, Lord!

"Was it long to you, dearest?" he queried, his dark face aflame. "To me — I have been a fool. Nothing should have kept me from you. To trust to messengers, letters — a fool — too late!" Silence. The hands unclasped; ties were broken. "Too late!" He turned bitterly away.

"Would that we had met in happier days!" she murmured sadly, making a brave effort at self-control.

"No reproaches, Lady Elizabeth," he answered, the touch of formality in the address showing his own equal strife. "What must be, must be! At least I have met you before I die, and for a year and a half I have thought of you, and dreamed of you, and held you the lady of my heart. E'en death itself cannot rob me of that sweet joy — for it is past."

They looked apart, and heard above the voice of the great deep, the unfathomable sound of the moaning surge far beneath them, chafing against the pebbles in the still morning, the wild beating of their hearts; after a little pause he continued more softly, —

LADY ELIZABETH

"And you — you will forget the young Irishman, the soldier of fortune, whom untoward fate threw across your pathway; and in your own English home, and in the love of your noble husband, may you be happy."

"Nay, not so," she said softly, taking his hand again, her eyes filling with tears; this time she was the stronger. "My heart is not made of such fickle stuff. I shall do my duty, keep my plighted word — even you would have me do no less than that — but not more steadfastly than I shall keep you within my recollection. But do not talk of death, you must not; I know the admiral — he has a kindly heart — "

"I would not live," replied the young man, quietly, "for life is death when the heart is dead."

"Tell me," asked the girl, nervously breaking the almost insupportable silence, "were you there when my mother's picture fell last night?"

"Yes, so near to it that it almost fell into my arms," he answered, smiling.

"A bad omen!" she murmured, shaking her head.

"What, that it should fall into my arms?"

"No, that it should fall at all."

"Well, I do not believe in omens, and 't is in the arms of another that you fall, at any rate. He gets the substance, I the shadow, the illusion — and even that is broken!"

"And so even the shadow is lost," said Elizabeth.

"Not yet. Open my heart, you will find it there," he answered quickly. "But how like you the portrait was!"

"Yes, I am said to look like my mother," she answered, striving, as we all do in tragic moments, to reach the height of the commonplace. "In the dress I now wear, under the changing fashions, the likeness is not so striking; but when I am gowned as she was, in the identical costume, which is still in existence, by the way, and sit as she did, in the dim light in that old chair, the resemblance is even more striking."

"Would that I might see you thus — in that dress of the olden time! Nothing except your actual presence in the hall has ever startled me so much as that image of the past did last night. You are so like the picture, but more beautiful, I think."

"Ah, yes, youth and the present are always the more beautiful. The admiral says I am not to be mentioned beside her — he loved her, I think — she was his cousin; they tell me she married very young, unhappily, too, and died when I was born, many years after. My father, too, died; I can scarcely remember him at all; I am alone."

"There should be a warning in this, should there not?" he asked softly; an idle question, fate had determined.

"I suppose so," replied the girl, wearily; "but what was I to do? The arrangement was made when I was a child. I have grown up with Edward Coventry, he loves me, he is a noble fellow, I respect — esteem him highly. It is a long-cherished wish of the admiral's; it was my mother's wish as well. I put him off, in spite of the engagement, for

LADY ELIZABETH

a year — for six months again," she said, with a glance the fond reproach of which cut him to the heart. "I promised him, on my word of honor, if he would only wait that time I would make no further objections. I cannot break that word now."

"Not even for me?"

"No, not even for you."

"But you do not love him?" he asked eagerly.

"Yes," she answered slowly; "I do — in a way, that is."

"But not like — "

"Enough, Lieutenant O'Neill!" she answered proudly, resuming, perforce, her erstwhile haughty air, which was belied by a deep flush on her cheeks. "'T is not generous of you to press me further. I — we have decided. I can stand no more. Forgive me — Have mercy!"

"I respect your decision; nay, more, I honor you for it, Lady Elizabeth," he answered gravely. "I kiss your hand and go to my death smiling. Forget me."

"Your death!" she cried in alarm. "What mean you?"

"The admiral, sir, would speak with you in the office at once," interrupted the sergeant, who had approached with a file of soldiers.

"You see — the summons," replied O'Neill, calmly, to Elizabeth. "Friend, I attend you — good-bye."

CHAPTER XI

O'Neill will keep his Honor

THE admiral had fully matured his plans during the night, and was prepared to make the assault upon the fortifications of O'Neill's honor at the most convenient season. In order to have a clear field for his operations, he had despatched his son upon an errand which would necessitate his absence until the evening. It had been with his full knowledge that his captive had been allowed to meet and converse with his ward. He trusted more to the fascinations of that young woman to effect his end, than to any other known agency, in fact.

Beauty and affection when allied have ever been most potent weapons, even when used to promote the cause of treachery and dishonor. Not that the admiral himself would have done anything he considered dishonorable. He would rather have cut off his right hand, which had done such stout service for his king, he would sacrifice his life, his son's life, anything, rather than jeopard it; but he would not hesitate to cajole the young Irishman into betraying his leader if he could. Though he should despise him if he acceded to the terms he would propose, yet he would not refrain from making use of him, even to his own undoing, if possible. 'T was the custom of war, and the obloquy which in similar instances has ever been heaped upon the tempted has not seemed to attach itself to the tempter under such conditions.

Still the admiral did not rejoice in the situation, and he could not make up his mind just how much it was necessary to offer. He had rather an uncomfortable feeling that he could go very far, and then not succeed after all; yet the greatness of the stake for which he played, he thought, would justify his action, for the person of John Paul Jones was certainly more coveted than that of any other man who had ever warred against the English flag. The governor had under his immediate command two excellent frigates, the Serapis, 44, and the Scarborough, 28; and if through his planning and foresight they should capture Jones and his ships, he might aspire to any honor in the gift of the king.

"Good-morning, my dear marquis," he said pleasantly, as soon as the young lieutenant was ushered into the office.

"Good-morning to your Lordship," answered O'Neill, bravely.

"I have sent for you to give you the run of the castle to-day," continued the admiral, much to his prisoner's surprise. "I shall be occupied with preparations rendered necessary by the advent of your friends the Americans, and urgent business required that I despatch your acquaintance, my son, on an errand which will keep him away until evening. Meanwhile, I leave you to the tender mercies of my ward, the Lady Elizabeth. In the evening I shall

THE GRIP OF HONOR

have something of great importance to say to you. You will give me your parole, of course, and I trust that you may have a pleasant day."

"In the presence of Lady Elizabeth, sir, all moments are hours of pleasure. I can never sufficiently thank you for your indulgence. You have crowned the victim with a chaplet of roses before offering him upon the altar," answered the bewildered officer. He suspected something; but in the thought of another day with his heart's desire, he resolutely put aside all other things — one day, in the strain of life, so much gained!

"Never mind about the altar now," said the admiral. "Enjoy the day, and perhaps the termination of it may fit its beginning."

Such a day as the two young people passed together comes not often in earthly calendars. There was one subject which was forbidden them by honor and discretion. They therefore talked of other things and thought only of that, and the restraint in which each was held made their true opinions as open to each other as the day itself. They wandered together about the castle walls, gazed out upon the sparkling sea, and allowed themselves to dream that the day would never end. They forgot the black future, and lived only in the fleeting moments of the present; 't is the habit of youth and love.

When the night fell they separated reluctantly, to meet again by her appointment in half an hour in the great hall, for what reason he knew not; that she wished it was sufficient for him. There had come

O'NEILL WILL KEEP HIS HONOR

into Elizabeth's head a quaint conceit. She wished to surprise him. As she left him she ran hastily to the ancient wardrobe in her private apartment in which, with the prudent forethought of our ancestors, her mother's wedding robe was laid away in sprigs of lavender. Hastily doffing her own garments, and assisted by the skilful fingers of her maid, she arrayed herself therein.

The body of the dress was of heavily brocaded white satin, worn over moderate hoops; the bodice was cut low and square across the neck and shoulders and terminated in a pointed stomacher of delicate pale blue, laced over the front with silver cord. The short, rather full sleeves edged with priceless lace left the sweet young arms bare to the dimpled elbow. The overdress or panier, looped with gold cord on either side, was of a fugitive shade of pale wild rose; the dress was lifted in front to show her dainty feet in their diamond-buckled, preposterously high-heeled, pointed-toed, blue satin shoes, and rose-colored, gold-clocked stockings. When she stood up, a little train swept the floor.

The old-fashioned waist of the gown was very *decolleté;* she blushed at the thought of it; but as it was in the picture, she draped it with delicate tulle, less white than her neck itself, and caught here and there by tiny diamond stars, and so she put it bravely on. To re-dress her hair was an easy matter; the low coiffure, with the hair unpowdered and rolled above her broad, low brow, after the style of the beautiful but venal Pompadour, and adorned with three delicate white ostrich tips, and with a string of pearls intertwined in its meshes, was most becoming. With eager hands rummaging among her mother's jewels, she soon found and twined the brilliant necklace of the picture about her throat; on her breast she pinned a great sunburst of diamonds, in the midst of which flashed a gleaming sapphire. A little black patch or two on her cheeks completed her preparations.

Then, full of anticipation for her lover, she ran down to the hall. To her great disappointment, the room was empty; he had not yet come. She waited a moment; her eyes fell upon the frame from which the remnants of the tattered painting had been removed, which was leaning on a dais in front of an alcove against the wall, just beneath the spot where the picture had hung. A new thought occurred to her. Why not? She eagerly pushed the old chair behind the frame, arranged it as it had been in the picture, and sat down in exactly the same position her mother had assumed when the portrait had been painted. She had often practised it before the mirror, and had acquired the pose perfectly.

The rich, dark old tapestry of Arras formed an appropriate background, and life and love and expectation threw a light in her eyes and painted upon her cheek hues that no skill, however cunning, could have duplicated, no palette save that of Nature in her rarest mood supplied. The girl had forgotten, for the moment, her engagement to another; she

O'NEILL WILL KEEP HIS HONOR

had forgotten the impending fate which hung over the man she truly loved. She was only a woman — loving — beloved — waiting. The thought of his surprise, the consciousness of her own beauty, deepened the color on her cheeks, and the palpitation of her bosom told of the beating of her heart.

She looked hastily about her, and, as the door opened, settled herself in the position of sweet repose of the picture. Never had earth borne a fairer woman. The first sound that struck her ear was the somewhat harsh voice of her guardian. A wave of disappointment swept across her. She half rose, as if to discover herself, and then, as she heard her lover's voice, she sank back and waited, motionless and expectant.

"Lieutenant Barry O'Neill, Marquis de Richemont, I bid you good evening," said the admiral, genially.

"Sir, good evening to you," replied O'Neill, something warning him of an impending struggle.

"Allow me," said the admiral, passing his snuff-box, from which both gentlemen helped themselves elaborately.

"I have here," continued the old man, drawing a piece of paper from the desk as they walked toward the centre of the room, neither of them noticing the picture at the moment, as it was behind them, "some account of the life and adventures of one Gerald O'Neill, sometime gentleman of the County Clare in Ireland, who rebelled against his gracious

Majesty King George II., of blessed memory, in the year 1745. His lands were escheated to the crown, his life forfeited. Unfortunately for us, and fortunately for him, he escaped to the continent, entered the service of Louis XV., and became — "

"You may spare me any further details, my Lord. I know them too well. He became a marshal of France and my father."

"Two great honors, surely," said the admiral, smiling pleasantly.

"I thank your Lordship for the compliment; pray proceed."

"I have here, also, a brief account of the history of another gentleman in whom I doubt not you are deeply interested."

"And that is — "

"One Barry O'Neill, Marquis de Richemont."

"Your very humble servant, sir."

"Your discrimination does you honor, marquis," said the admiral, playfully.

"Faith, sir, you read me an easy riddle."

"I find that you have been concerned in every treasonable plot against his Majesty which has been hatched on the continent since you were out of leading strings."

"Rather hard, but true, sir. An Irishman, you know, is naturally a rebel and a conspirator."

"Quite so; and those who are not drowned may expect to be hanged," said the admiral, sternly.

"As I am a sailor, I might reasonably have hoped for the former end, but I have forfeited my rights by coming on shore, I suppose." He paused, and as the admiral nodded gravely, he continued with well-simulated indifference: "'T is not a pleasant mode of death, my Lord, nor one that I would have chosen, nor one that is becoming a gentleman; but I trust I shall meet it with equanimity at least," replied O'Neill, a little paler than before, but still dauntlessly smiling.

"I am glad to see that you are a man of such resolution, sir," said the admiral. "If your discretion equal your courage, the matter may be arranged."

"It is useless to try it," was the reply; "to have known your ward, to have seen her, and to know that she is destined for the arms of another, makes life a hell, and death a pleasure."

"Is it so?" said the admiral, pausing.

"Think of the days of your own youth, sir, and one that you loved, and you will understand me."

The admiral reflected. The stake he was playing for was so high, his desire was so great — like the woman who hesitated, he fell. There would be some way out of it, surely. As he drew near to the moment and to the goal, his overwhelming desire took possession of him, and blinded him; desire blinds as well as love.

"Even that," finally he said slowly, looking meaningly at O'Neill the while, "may be arranged."

"Good God!" said O'Neill, white to the lips. "What is it you would have me do? Speak! Titles, rank, station, friends, fame, opportunities, life itself, would I cheerfully give for her who has taken possession of me. Speak, my Lord!" cried the young man, entreatingly.

The heart of the girl in the picture frame in the dark corner stopped its beating. The gates of heaven, as it were, had been opened before her. What was the proposition?

"Listen!" said the admiral, slowly, at last. He was sure he had him now.

"I could settle the course of the world while I wait for your reply, sir. Delay no longer, I pray you; I am in a torture of apprehension," said O'Neill, eagerly.

"I design not to take from you rank nor station nor lands nor position," replied the admiral. "I offer you a free pardon for all your past offences; nay, it shall cover your father's as well, if you wish. There shall be a restoration of the ancient lands of your venerable house. I will put your feet upon a ladder by which you may rise to the very highest position. I open before you vistas of honorable advancement in the service of your rightful king in your native land, in which there is no limit to which a man of courage may not attain."

"These are nothing," said the young man, impetuously, "beside Lady Elizabeth Howard; some of the things you mention I now have, some I do not wish, some are nothing to me. But your ward, sir, what of her?"

"Oh, what a lover is there!" whispered to herself the girl in the picture frame, forgetting the pose, clasping her white hands and leaning forward with shining eyes, blushing cheeks, and parted lips, listening with wildly beating heart. This in her breast now was love, indeed, — in no way like to the pale affection with which she regarded the unfortunate Coventry. The admiral spoke again, fixing his eye upon the young man. His words came slowly.

"Well, sir, I will even agree to interpose no objections to your suit for the hand of my ward."

"But that is tantamount to giving your consent, my Lord," said O'Neill, coming nearer to him in great surprise, his heart bounding — and yet there must be some conditions to the royal gift. The admiral bowed. "And Major Coventry?" cried the Irishman.

"His desires must give way to — er — reasons of state," said the admiral, decisively. "I will arrange all that; if you can obtain her consent to your suit, she is yours, provided —" he paused significantly. Ah! the conditions!

"My consent!" thought Elizabeth, happiness flooding her like a wave; and then she remembered that she was a woman, and indignation found a lodgement in her being. 'Twas not thus she would be wooed and won, not in this bartering way disposed of. By what right did any one — even her guardian — presume to — O'Neill was speaking again.

"What are the conditions — what is it you wish me to do? If it be in human power, 'tis done. Torment me no more; as you are a man and have a heart, speak!" In his agitation the younger man seized the elder by the arm.

THE GRIP OF HONOR

"I desire you to go back to your ship and arrange to put in my possession the person of John Paul Jones," said the admiral, with the greatest deliberation, concealing his anxiety by an appearance of great firmness, as he nonchalantly helped himself to a pinch of snuff. An accurate observer would have noticed that the trembling of his hands belied his simulated calmness.

It was out now! What would the man say or do? Elizabeth sank back appalled. So this was the condition; this was the test. He was to choose between her and black treachery — dishonor! His answer, what would it be? Had her idol feet of clay, after all? Her fate hung in the balance; she could never survive his shame if he fell; if not — ah!

O'Neill released the admiral at once, stared at him a long moment in horrified silence, shrank away from him, and sank down in the chair and buried his face in his hands for a little space; his two auditors waited, hope for different results trembling in either heart. Presently he looked up and rose to his feet.

"Treachery — dishonor — shame! And with her innocence and youth and beauty you bait your trap!" ejaculated O'Neill, brokenly. The admiral still played with his snuff-box, his eyes averted, his hands trembling still. Was it age, or —

"Oh, my God, my God!" continued the sailor, stricken to the very heart, "to raise my hopes to such a pitch — to put the cup of happiness to my very lips — to open the gates of heaven in my very

O'NEILL WILL KEEP HIS HONOR

presence — and couple your propositions with this — this infamy! I am a lover, sir, you know it well; but you should not have forgotten that I am, before everything else, a gentleman. How could you do it? It ill becomes your years," he went on impetuously, in mounting indignation. "I am your prisoner — your captive; but I knew not that misfortune gave you a right to insult me thus My Lord, my Lord, the ladder upon which you put my feet leads down, not up; hell, not heaven, is its end!"

"Think!" said the admiral, doggedly, feeling the game was lost, but, like a desperate gamester, playing on. "The Lady Elizabeth is at the end, wher-e'er it be."

"I love her, God only knows how much I love her; from the moment I saw her I have had no thought but for her. I could not look her in the face and be guilty of this thing." The girl in the picture almost cried aloud for joy in this triumph of her lover's honor.

"She shall never know," replied the admiral. "I will pledge my word of honor."

The honor of the tempter, for the dishonor of the tempted! O'Neill laughed bitterly.

"It has not in forty years of service been called in question," replied the old man, stifling his growing shame.

"Nor has mine," said O'Neill, "until this hour. You are her guardian — an old man — your gray hairs should protect you; but 't is well for you that I have no sword, for I swear I would plunge it first into your heart and then into my own!"

"Think what it is I offer," persisted the other. "Compare it to what you now have in the way of worldly honor. What do you care for that bit of striped bunting and those beggarly rebels who have presumed to declare a republic? What is a republic, anyway, and what function has it in a gentleman's life, pray? What have we to do with the common people? What are their aspirations to you? What affiliations have you for that low-born gardener, turned pirate and buccaneer to ravage our coasts, dishonor our flag? This is the kingdom in which you were born. Here your rightful allegiance is due. I offer you, for the giving up of a — sentiment which possesses you, the favor of your king and the hand of the woman you love, — every earthly thing to make you happy. You are an exile, a wanderer, a soldier of fortune. I give you a country again."

"And do you, a man of honor, advise me to — "

"Damnation, sir! I advise nothing, I offer; the decision rests with you."

"Ah, I thought so; and what would you do in my place, sir?"

"I'm not there, thank God!" said the old man, fervently; "and I repeat, you must decide yourself."

"Very good, sir. It is true that I like not that republic, its principles are nothing to me; but I have found that gardener's son a man — ay, a gentleman! You have called me a landless man, an exile,

O'NEILL WILL KEEP HIS HONOR

a soldier of fortune, — that, too, is true. But to Captain Jones and his service I have pledged my honor; 't is all I have; the stars and stripes are become my flag; I wear the uniform, I eat the bread, of the United States. You may break my heart, destroy my life; you cannot break my word. There is not power and place enough in the three kingdoms, no, not even on their throne, not beauty enough even in Elizabeth Howard to tempt me — to compel me to do that. Say no more. You have your answer."

CHAPTER XII

Gentlemen All

"LOOK, you fool!" said the admiral, roughly, furious with rage at being balked in this way, though, in spite of himself, his heart exulted in the nobility of the man. "Look, you beggarly Irishman!" he exclaimed, turning the surprised young man about before he could recover himself, — "look on the picture of her whom you reject! Gaze upon it! If you love her, say whether or no your high-flown sentiments of honor can stand against that prospect." It was his final appeal, win or lose; he had staked all upon the throw.

There in the great frame stood the most beautiful picture that the eyes of either man had ever seen. Elizabeth was standing. One tiny hand clutched tightly her heaving bosom; the other arm was stretched out with upraised palm like a goddess in command. The light of the flickering candles cast subtle shadows upon her face. The dusk of the room intensified the illusion and spiritualized her beauty. O'Neill looked at her with all his life in his gaze; so glorious, so splendid, so perfect a creature would shake the very soul of honor itself!

The admiral had played his last card; this was the end of his resource, and he watched the Irish-

He watched her in awe-struck silence, sank on his knees, stretched out his arms.

GENTLEMEN ALL

man with all the intensity of a tiger about to spring on its prey. The moments fled. He knew that he had lost. Elizabeth had risen in the stress of her anxiety, the strain had been too much for her; she had been about to intervene between them, when the glances of the two men arrested her step. She waited, one little foot outstretched, her body leaning forward slightly, a picture of triumph, her eyes as two lambent flames playing upon her lover. He watched her in awestruck silence, sank on his knees, stretched out his arms, murmuring softly, —

"Thou knowest that I love thee. I have dreamed sometimes that in happier days thou mightest have given me thy heart, but I could not take it with a bar sinister of shame between us! No — " Was she moving! Was that some trick of the wavering light!

"Good heavens!" cried O'Neill, fearfully, rising. "See — is it a spirit? She shakes her head! Look you, my Lord, she is alive; the picture fell last night, you remember — 'T is herself! Elizabeth, Elizabeth, you have heard and seen — have I not decided well?"

"How dare you, my Lord!" exclaimed the girl, coming down from the dais and stepping swiftly toward the astonished admiral, who shrank back from her, — "how dare you make my hand the reward of treachery; my person the bait for dishonor? And by what right do you dispose of me without consulting me? Am I a slave, that you force me upon this gentleman? My word is given

THE GRIP OF HONOR

to your son; you yourself insisted upon it. You would play the traitor double, and would fain make him do the same. And for what? To compass the death of one poor man to whom I owe life and honor, who is only fighting for what he calls his freedom! Shame upon your gray hairs, sir! Oh, the insult to my modesty — to be thus bandied about between two men — And you, sir!" she cried, in tempestuous passion, turning to O'Neill, — "you do me the honor to refuse me — to reject me — me — me — Elizabeth Howard — look at me — you would have none of me — "

"My honor — " cried O'Neill, amazed at her sudden change and inconsistency.

"Your honor — have I any honor, sir? Would you have left me a shadow of it between you? Stand back, sir! My Lord, is it thus you discharge the trust committed to you by my mother? To give this gentleman opportunity to return to France, and say that he has refused my hand?"

"He shall not go back to France, Lady Elizabeth," said the admiral, sternly.

"Why not, pray?" asked Elizabeth, faltering, her passionate anger checked by the admiral's word and look.

"Because he shall be tried and hanged to-morrow as an American spy or a captured traitor, whichever he may elect."

She stood as if petrified at these cruel words.

"It is right, sir," said O'Neill. "I submit; and if you would make me die happy, say that the

GENTLEMEN ALL

hideous proposition I have had from you was but the test of my honor."

"Oh, sir!" cried Elizabeth, in agony, throwing herself upon her knees before the admiral, "forgive me for my wild, intemperate speech; I know not what I say. You have been a father to me from the beginning, and I have ever loved you as one; I have turned to you for everything. Unsay your cruel words! Retract this order! You cannot condemn this honest gentleman. Dispose of me as you will. I love him — I love him — ay, let the truth be heard — even for his rejection of me! Nay, had he not done so, I would have hated him. Spare his life — I will marry Edward, do anything you wish — grant me this boon!"

"I cannot," said the admiral, slowly; "I pity you, from my soul I do, and him as well, but I dare not. There is but one thing that would excuse my clemency to his Majesty — there is the alternative he has nobly rejected: die he must, or give up his captain!"

"A thousand deaths rather than that!" answered O'Neill. "Rise, Lady Elizabeth; your appeal is vain. Rejoicing in your approval of my action, thankful to God that I have heard you say, 'I love you,' I shall die happy."

"No, no!" said the girl, spreading her arms protectingly before him, and then throwing herself upon his breast, "you cannot die — you shall not die! Oh, my love, my love, I knew not until I heard you speak what this feeling was. I cannot let you go! Surely, you would never be so cruel as to part us now?" she cried brokenly, looking back at the impassive old man; his hands were steady enough now, — they never trembled but from shame. "What has he done? He came here to see me, — me alone, — to take me in his arms as he holds me now; and you condemn him to death for that! Did you never love when you were young? They whispered that it was my mother who had your heart. They told me that she was unhappy because they forced you apart. 'T was to you she confided me. Have pity, in her name, have mercy!"

"Enough!" said the admiral; "it is not that I will not, but I cannot. He has chosen; he must die."

"Then may death come to me," said Elizabeth; "because, for all eternity, I love him!"

"And this," broke in the cold, stern voice of Major Coventry, who had entered the room at that moment, "is the welcome I receive from my bride of to-morrow, and this is the reward of the efforts I have made to secure the release of the Marquis de Richemont, my friend! May God have pity on me, — my sweetheart and my friend!"

"Sir!" said O'Neill, brokenly, "I crave your forgiveness. I knew that she was yours — I do not understand how we got into this position," passing his hand over his forehead in bewilderment; "but this I know, — I am to die! There is no choice. She will yet be yours."

"Never — never!" cried Elizabeth, turning **to**

him. "Edward, if you have truly loved me, — if I have rightly estimated you, your nobility of soul, your generosity of heart, — you will plead for us with your father. You will give me up; you are too proud to take an unwilling bride, and one who in spite of herself — for I have fought against it for your sake — confesses that she loves another. You will intercede with your father — I will bless you all the days of my life. Edward, Edward, the companion of my childhood's hours — my friend — my brother — my only hope is in you! Speak!" She fell at his feet and clasped his hand, which she covered with kisses. There was another silence. Coventry covered his face with his other hand; the sweat of agony bedewed his brow.

"Rise, Elizabeth, you shall not put your trust in me in vain," he cried hoarsely, at last. "Father, can nothing be done? I will not stand in the way."

"My son — Lady Elizabeth — Lieutenant O'Neill — there is nothing that can be done. My duty is perfectly clear. The only possible salvation of the prisoner would be in the action which he has refused even to consider; and, sir, if it were my duty to effect, if possible, the capture of your captain and his ship through you, I can only say that I am glad that I have failed. I apologize to you; you are a man of honor, indeed, sir. I know few who would have resisted such a plea as this. Say no more, Elizabeth, it is not that I will not — I cannot! Edward, here is my seal. Make out the warrant for an order for a court-martial to-morrow morning; it is a necessary form, of course. The execution of Lieutenant O'Neill will follow at once." Elizabeth did not faint, — no, not yet; there would be time for that later. She clung to O'Neill and listened.

"What shall be the manner of my death, sir?" queried the latter.

"Hanging, sir. 'T is the penalty prescribed by the law."

"It is a poor death for a man, my Lord, but 't will serve. A last request, sir. I am a sailor — may I be hanged upon a ship?" he asked again, pressing the trembling woman to his breast.

"I grant that — would that I could grant more! Major Coventry, you will direct Captain Pearson of the Serapis to execute the sentence of the court, which will meet on his ship, the prisoner to be confined there meanwhile. You will find the papers in the library; here is my seal; hasten, and get the painful matter over." Coventry left the room at once, in obedience to his orders.

"And at what time, sir, will the sentence be carried out?" asked O'Neill, Elizabeth still clinging to him, covering him with incoherent caresses, and fighting against despair.

"To-morrow evening at half after six o'clock."

"Very well, my Lord."

At this moment the old sergeant entered the room and saluted the admiral.

"A French officer, wich he says he's from the

GENTLEMEN ALL

American Continental squadron, has come ashore in a small cutter, under a flag of truce, an' desires to speak with your Lordship. He asks for a safe-conduct."

"Tell him he shall return as freely as he came, on the word of a British officer, and admit him."

A slender, dapper little man, in the brilliant uniform of a French marine officer, his head covered with a powdered wig, entered the room a moment later, and bowed profoundly. Elizabeth started violently as she beheld him.

"Whom have I the honor of addressing?" asked the admiral.

"The Vicomte de Chamillard, a colonel of marines in the navy of France, serving as a volunteer in the American squadron," was the reply.

"And you come on behalf of —"

"Captain John Paul Jones, to protest against your unlawful detention of another French officer, the Marquis de Richemont, my Lord."

"He is a spy, caught in the very act: he has admitted it; and if that were not enough, I find he is an attainted traitor. A court is ordered for tomorrow morning on the Serapis; his execution, which will be inevitable, is set for half after six o'clock in the evening; he shall hang from one of the frigate's yard-arms."

"De Chamillard," said O'Neill, "you can do nothing."

"The laws of war —" persisted the Frenchman.

"It is in accordance with those laws that I do

what I do," replied the admiral, shortly; "and you may say to your captain that if I catch him he shall swing from the first yard-arm that comes in the harbor."

"I am answered, then. Very good; I shall remember your courteous words, my Lord; and now I enter my formal protest against this unwarranted action on your part concerning the Marquis de Richemont. The King of France will have something to say about it. I bid you farewell."

"Farewell, sir," said the admiral, indifferently turning away.

"De Richemont, good-bye; embrace me." As the two men came together, the Frenchman whispered, "This woman — is she your friend?"

"Yes," replied O'Neill, quickly.

"Mademoiselle," said De Chamillard, turning to Elizabeth with a keen look in his eyes. Recognizing him at last, she stretched out her hand to him. He murmured as he bent low over it, "Delay the execution for at least six hours, and I will save him." Elizabeth sank down in her chair, a gleam of hope in her heart.

"I salute you," he said, turning away.

"Sergeant," cried the admiral, "attend the Vicomte de Chamillard and see him safely bestowed on his vessel."

As the Frenchman turned toward the door, he came face to face with Major Coventry returning with the orders he had prepared.

"Paul Jones, by Heaven!" shouted the latter.

GENTLEMEN ALL

"At your service," said the supposed Frenchman, promptly tearing off his wig and laying his hand on his sword.

"Ha!" cried the admiral. "Have you dared to come here! I have you now! Call the guard! Sergeant, arrest this rebel — this traitor — this pirate — disarm him! You shall never leave this castle but for the ship, sir. The yard-arm is there."

"Stop, my Lord!" answered Jones, calmly, as the men crowded toward him; "stand back, sergeant, back, men! You cannot touch me; I have that which will protect me wherever flies the English flag."

"And that is — " said the admiral, smiling contemptuously.

"Your word, sir, — the word of an English officer."

The old man bit his lip in chagrined silence. He struggled with himself, looking at the easy, *insouciant* Scotsman before him.

"In seventy years it has not been broken," he said at last. "Well for you that you secured it. Go! You are free! You are a bold man, sir, but, I warn you, do not cross my path again."

"I am proud to have met so true a gentleman. Will you honor me?" said Paul Jones, presenting his snuff-box to the admiral. The old man hesitated, laughed in spite of himself, and finally helped himself to a pinch.

"The d——d insolence of the man!" he exclaimed. "I'd like to have met you in my young days, yard-arm to yard-arm."

"I would have endeavored to occupy you, sir," said Jones, coolly; "and now I bid you farewell."

He shot one meaning glance at Elizabeth, and his lips seemed to form the words "six hours," as he departed from the room.

"Here is the warrant, sir," said Coventry. "Again I ask, and this time I ask my father, can nothing be done?"

"Nothing, sir, less as a father than in any other capacity. Sergeant, take your prisoner. Major Coventry, you will conduct him on the Serapis, and remain there as my representative until the execution is over. Sir, you have borne yourself well this day; I would shake you by the hand. Good-bye."

O'Neill clasped the proffered hand warmly, and then looked from Coventry, standing erect, immovable, white-faced, to Elizabeth, who was still sitting with bowed head, a world of entreaty in his glance. Coventry nodded and turned away. O'Neill stepped quickly to the girl's side, took her hand in his, bowed low over it, pressed a long kiss upon it.

"May you be happy!" he said. "Farewell!"

She looked at him in dazed silence.

"Sir," he continued, turning back to Coventry, and saluting him, "I am ready. Lead on."

"Forward, march, sergeant!" commanded the officer, hoarsely, and with no backward look the little cortége moved from the room. The girl rose to her feet as if to start after them, but the old man restrained her.

"O'Neill — O'Neill — " rang through the hall — a wild, despairing cry — and then Lady Elizabeth sank down white and still at the feet of the admiral.

"And this is love!" he murmured, shaking his old head; "I had forgotten it."

BOOK III

ON THE VERGE OF ETERNITY

CHAPTER XIII

A Desperate Move

IT was morning when Elizabeth came again to the terrace above the water battery overlooking the harbor. She had passed a night of sleepless agony, and her pallid face, with its haggard expression, the great black circles under the eyes, — for her grief had been too deep for tears, — gave outward evidence of her breaking heart. She had besought the admiral again and again to stay the execution of her lover, urging every plea that the most desperate mind could suggest; she had implored his mercy and pity upon every ground, and upon his inexorable refusal had begged that he might be reprieved for a few hours, and that she might at least be allowed to see him before he died. Touched by her sorrow, at first the old man had been inclined to grant this petition, and had scribbled a line on his official paper, giving the desired permission; but before he signed and sealed it, he changed his mind, and deemed it best to refuse, — more merciful to her, in fact.

It really wrung his heart to be unable to extend clemency to this young man. He repented him of the temptation he had thrown in his way. The nobility with which O'Neill had refused and rejected the chance of life which had been offered him, the simplicity with which he had given up everything for honor, impressed him more than ever. He was sick at heart at the grief of his ward, whom he truly loved, and the broken, despairing face of his son, since he had learned that Elizabeth loved O'Neill, haunted him. He wished that the Irishman had never come across his path, though he could not but admire his honor, his grace, and his courage. He was bitterly sorry that he had ever attempted to influence the man; he had an uncomfortable and growing suspicion that his plans had brought nothing but trouble to every one. Breaking away from the presence of Elizabeth, whose anguished face was a living reproach to him, he finally secluded himself in his office and refused to see her again.

So the day, like yesterday, wore away; but, oh, how differently! The girl never knew how she passed the hours. She wandered restlessly up and down the terrace, her eyes strained upon the sea. The garrison, who idolized her to a man, had been apprised by the sergeant of what had happened, and, to a man, they were upon her side. The men would never forget the picture she made, as they watched her pacing to and fro, ceaselessly gazing at the white ship in the harbor, — her lover's prison, his scaffold even.

The sense of impotent helplessness with which she was compelled to face the situation, the knowledge that O'Neill was doomed absolutely, that there was nothing that she could do or say which would alter the decision, was terrible. She had been

A DESPERATE MOVE

accustomed to have her will, and like most women loved it. Now she had to stand by in the bright sunlight with all the strength of life and youth and love in her veins and in his, and see her lover choked to death — hanged like a dog — at the black yard-arm of that great ship yonder.

And for what? Womanlike, she put aside every thought of him but that he had dared death itself only to see her, to be in her presence again! Oh, how splendid, how handsome, how noble he had been in the great hall, when he had refused her rather than to take her as the reward of treachery! and now he was to become a lifeless lump of clay, alive to her only as a memory, a recollection — how cruel! She could not, she would not, stand it. She racked her brain over and over. Was there nothing? No —

It was late in the afternoon. Her maid had not been able to drag her from the terrace whence she had a view of the ship on which her lover was to be executed, — murdered, she said. As she gazed upon it, she noticed two men climbing nimbly up the black shrouds about the foremast. When they reached the foreyard, they ran out on the yard-arm. One of them carried something. A rope was dragging from it. In obedience to an imperious command, her maid ran and fetched her a glass. One look through it showed her — she was a sailor's ward — that they were rigging a whip on the yard-arm, they were securing there a girt-line block through which a rope was rove, leading to the top and thence to the deck. She divined at once its hideous pur

THE GRIP OF HONOR

pose. The hour! The hour! Had it grown so late? Was it so near, so near? Was there a God in that blue heaven bending above her head? Could such things be?

A sick feeling came over her heart, and she would have fainted but for a sudden inspiration. Again she seized the telescope, — an unusually strong one, by the way, — and raising it to her eyes with unsteady hand, eagerly swept the sea off in the direction of Flamborough Head, rising faintly down to the southward, a long distance away. For a long time her nervous, trembling hands could not get that part of the horizon in focus. She finally knelt down and rested the tube upon the parapet, breathing a prayer as she did so, and looked again.

Ah! At last she had it, and there swept into the field of vision three gleams of white on the skyline, proclaiming, even to her unpractised eye, the sails of ships! What had that indomitable man said to her last night in the hall?

"Delay the execution for at least six hours, and I will save him!" He was not one to promise lightly. She would try again. The telescope fell with a crash at her feet.

She would make one more appeal to the admiral; it was late, but there might yet be time. On the instant she turned, leaving the startled maid, and ran like a fleet-footed fawn along the terrace, down the stone steps through the water battery, through the bailey, into the inner court, down the long passage, and into the great hall of the night before,

A DESPERATE MOVE

where the admiral was usually to be found at this hour. She dashed impetuously into the room, crying, —

"The admiral, quick! where is he?"

"Ships has been reported down at Bridlin'ton Bay, — furrin ships, yer Leddyship," replied the old sergeant, who happened to be there alone, "an' his Ludship took horse about half-past twelve o'clock to go down there."

Failure! Her last hope gone! She sank down into the chair. Reaction had come; she was fainting, helpless, dying. It was over! The sergeant started toward her, his face full of pity. She was sitting in the admiral's chair, by the great table. Her glance fell listlessly upon it. At the moment another idea flashed into her mind. Desperate, foolish, nevertheless, she would try it — try anything; this, at least, was action. She started to her feet again on the instant, instinct with life.

"Leave me at once, and see that no one interrupts me; I wish to be alone," she said imperiously to the astonished sergeant, who bowed respectfully and withdrew. A half an hour later she came hurriedly out of the room, white-faced, drawn, nerved up to desperate endeavor.

How he got through the night, O'Neill never knew. The court-martial in the morning had taken little time; its sentence, a foregone conclusion, promptly approved by the admiral, had been death by hanging at half after six o'clock that night. He

THE GRIP OF HONOR

had refused to give any further parole, in the faint hope that something might enable him to escape, and consequently had been heavily ironed and placed in confinement in the space between two of the great guns on the lower gun-deck — the Serapis was a double-banked frigate — on the starboard side. The forethought of Coventry, who had attended him with the solicitude and kindness of a brother, and had pleaded for him unavailingly before the court, had caused a canvas screen to be provided, which enclosed two of the guns, and allowed him to pass his hours undisturbed by the curious gaze of the English seamen. An armed marine stood always as sentry before the screen.

Captain Pearson, a gallant officer, had been kindness itself in all his arrangements, but his orders, which were peremptory, left him no discretion whatever. O'Neill passed his time sitting by the open port, leaning on a gun, gazing out over the water at the gray old castle where he had found his love and met his fate. Many tragedies had been enacted within its walls during long centuries of history — none sadder than his own.

It would have been foolish to say that he had no regrets. No one could think of the possibilities of happiness presented by such a love as that which he was now assured Elizabeth felt for him, without a sense of despair coming over the mind in the knowledge they were not to be enjoyed; but he was a sailor, and generations of heroic ancestors had accustomed him to look death in the face,

A DESPERATE MOVE

and smile undaunted at its harsh, forbidding appearance.

"*Fortune, Infortune, Fortune,*" had been the motto of his branch of the red-handed O'Neills; at least that was the punning Latin translation of a Celtic original which meant, "Fortune and misfortune are alike to the strong."

When his friends and acquaintances at the French court, those knights and ladies with whom he had ruffled it so bravely, the young king, his master, his old comrades, the hard fighters on the Richard, her dauntless captain, that brave old man, his father, heard how he died, they would learn that he had met the last grim enemy with the wonted intrepidity of his race. *Noblesse oblige!* and then having made his peace with God as best he could alone, — he was of a different faith from that of the chaplain of the ship, — he gave himself over to mournful dreams of Elizabeth Howard.

Late in the afternoon his meditations were interrupted by the arrival of Coventry. The poignant unhappiness of the young Englishman was, if anything, greater than that of O'Neill. His engagement to Elizabeth Howard, with whom he had grown up, had been at first more or less a matter of convenience, and he had never entirely realized the hold she had taken upon his heart, until he heard her — in the arms of O'Neill — make that frantic avowal of her overwhelming passion. Men frequently do not know the value of what they have — until they lose it.

THE GRIP OF HONOR

Coventry's heart had been surcharged with love and devotion to this woman, and because his life had glided on evenly he had not known how full of love it was until he had been so shaken that it had overflowed. He would, he thought, cheerfully have taken the other's place, sentence of death and all, could he hear but once before he died the ringing accents of such a sublime confession — and for himself. His love for the woman of his choice was of the most exalted character, and might well, were merit or fitness alone to be considered in such a case, have claimed her own deepest feelings in return.

When Elizabeth had appealed to him to intervene, with a magnanimity as rare as it was noble, he had subordinated his happiness to her own, and had endeavored to procure a mitigation of the punishment imposed upon his rival, though he knew his success would throw his promised wife into the arms of O'Neill. He had not done this without a terrible struggle, — it was a gray-faced, broken man who looked upon the world of to-day, in place of the smiling youth of the night before, — but he had done it. He felt that the sacrifice would cost him his life, and for that he was truly glad, yet he had offered it freely, generously, and nobly. He had not hesitated to do so, for with him the happiness of Elizabeth Howard was the paramount passion.

If she did not love him, he could at least show her what love truly meant in its highest sense; give her a lesson in love like to the lesson in honor that

A DESPERATE MOVE

other man had exhibited last night. For her he stood ready to give up everything; his own future he did not allow to weigh a moment in the balance beside hers.

There was something grandly sublime in this utter abnegation of self, so simply done for another's happiness. Coventry had been a Christian after a rather better fashion, perhaps, than most young men of his time; his associations with the sweet, pure girl he loved had kept him so. All his people for generations had been Churchmen; this seemed to him to be the right thing to do, the thing demanded of a gentleman; the greatest Gentleman of them all, who had shown His breeding on a Cross, had set the example of self-sacrifice. A sentence quoted by the chaplain in the service a few days before, which had struck his fancy, ran in his head; he had a good memory.

"*I will very gladly spend and be spent for you; though the more abundantly I love you, the less I be loved.*"

Yes, that was it.

At the first moment, when he found last night that his pleadings were of no avail, and that O'Neill was doomed to die, his heart had leaped in his breast at the thought that his rival would be removed; but he had crushed the thought as unworthy a gentleman of his high ideals; and there had come to him, in addition, a consciousness that to a love like Elizabeth Howard's the death of a beloved would make no change. Such passions come but once in a lifetime, and when they arrive they are as eternal as the stars. He had given her up, and she belonged, in life or death, to another. A glance at his own anguished heart enabled him to feel for her. Time would not soften a blow to a nature like to hers.

In the execution of O'Neill, Coventry saw the death-warrant of Elizabeth. He had passed the day racking his brain and thinking of some way to delay the execution, but without avail. He would have stopped at nothing to save them both. In despair he had come to consult with his rival.

CHAPTER XIV

Almost the End

"I AM glad to see you, my friend," said O'Neill, smiling at him in a melancholy way.

"Would God that I could see you in any place but this!" answered the young Englishman.

"Ah, yes!" replied O'Neill, his eyes brightening; "then we might fight it out, man to man, sword to sword, and —"

"Not so," mournfully replied Coventry. "The battle has been fought, and you have won again. Whether you live or die, Elizabeth Howard is not for me."

"My poor friend, may the day upon which I crossed your paths be accursed! I have brought to each of you nothing but sorrow," replied the young sailor, sadly, touched at the other's surrender.

"It was fate, O'Neill. Do not reproach yourself with that. All day long I have been striving to think of some means to delay this accursed execution, until I could communicate with the king. An appeal to his clemency might — but no — I see no way, nothing, unless — you know —" he hesitated and hung his head, blushing painfully.

"No more of that, if you love me, Coventry," said O'Neill, gravely. "Put yourself in my place!

THE GRIP OF HONOR

Could you do it? Ah, you shake your head, you see! Neither could I, not even to purchase heaven." There was a long pause between them.

"O'Neill," said the Englishman at last, "would that I could take your place!"

"But you cannot, Major Coventry," replied the other, gratefully. "You honor me in the thought; but if you could, I should refuse to allow it. You are the better man; all my life I have been a gay, reckless, pleasure-seeking soldier of fortune, with never a serious purpose until now, and now it is too late! You are the worthy one, and you must live to watch over, to care for her whom we both love. Perhaps — surely — in days to come she will forget; time, absence, you know — she will reward your devotion, she must — you will be happy — " His voice broke, and he turned away his face and looked out of the open port. Coventry shook his head.

"You know her not, sir. She is not for me, nor would I take her loving you; my love is too deep for that — nor would she come. She will never forget you." O'Neill's heart leaped at this assurance.

The ship's bell on the deck above them struck four times; it was six o'clock! There was a little silence within the screen.

"The hour approaches," said O'Neill, softly, at last. "I would be alone for a few moments before — you understand?"

"Yes," said the other, rising and pressing his hand. "Have you nothing to say, no message to send to — " he asked magnanimously.

ALMOST THE END

"Nothing — nothing — 't is best so. You will come for me at the time?"

"Yes, and I will stand by you to the end, like a soldier."

"You do me great honor," replied the other, thankfully. Coventry looked at him a moment, shook his head, and turned away.

In the prayers of the young Irishman the face of the girl he loved would obtrude itself. It seemed but a moment before he heard the tramp of armed men coming along the deck. They stopped before the screen. It was opened, and Coventry, pale as death, presented himself at the opening; the screen was promptly folded back; there were marines fully armed before it, the chaplain, too, in the white robes of his office.

"I am ready, gentlemen," said O'Neill, calmly. "May I not go to my death unbound?" he asked.

At a nod from Coventry, the master-at-arms unlocked the fetters about his feet and hands. The prisoner took his place in the midst of the little squad of men, and ascended to the spar-deck. The ship's company of marines was drawn up aft on the quarter-deck. Most of the seamen of the crew were arranged in orderly ranks in the starboard gangway. Forward a grating had been rigged on the bulwarks under the port fore-yard-arm. A new rope led from the grating, up through the block in the yard-arm, came inboard to another block under the top, and thence through a block fixed to the deck. Some sixty or seventy men chosen by lot from the ship's

THE GRIP OF HONOR

company had hold of the rope which was led aft along the port gangway. In front of the marines stood Captain Pearson and his officers in full uniform. The prisoner was halted before him.

"Are you aware, sir," said the captain, gravely, "that the hour for the carrying out of the sentence of the court approaches?"

"Yes, sir," answered O'Neill, courteously.

"Have you anything to say before that time?"

"I have to thank you all for your kindness to me, nothing else, sir."

"Allow me, sir," said the captain, "to assure you of the great personal distaste and regret I feel at being compelled to take this action."

"Your feelings do you honor, sir," replied O'Neill, gravely; "but it is a matter of duty. Pray, proceed."

"Captain Pearson," said Coventry, in great agitation, "can nothing be done to delay this execution a few hours? There are considerations, sir, in my possession, which I feel sure would incline his Majesty, could he be communicated with, to extend clemency to this gentleman, — circumstances which — "

"Are these circumstances within the knowledge of Lord Westbrooke, Major Coventry?" answered the captain, surprised at the unusual nature of the interruption.

"They are, sir."

"Have you mentioned them to him? Have you called his attention specifically to them, I mean?"

ALMOST THE END

"Yes, sir, I have," answered the soldier, reluctantly.

"And they have evidently not influenced him, you see. Therefore I fail to see how I can permit them to weigh with me."

"But a delay, sir, of a day, of an hour even, until I can communicate with the admiral again! For God's sake, sir, do not hang this gentleman like—"

"Major Coventry, you are a soldier, and should not make such an appeal. I have my orders. You have shown me no cause to disregard them; I cannot take it upon myself to do so. I dare not!"

"But an hour, sir, until I—"

"Not a moment! At five bells they must be carried out," said the captain, inflexibly. "No more, sir," he added, as Coventry made an impetuous step forward. "I have indulged you too long already. Mr. Pascoe, take the prisoner forward."

"It is useless, Coventry. Why prolong this agony longer? You have done what you could. I thank you and bless you," said O'Neill, as they walked along the deck to the place of the grating.

"Will you please to step up here, sir?" said Pascoe, the first lieutenant of the Serapis, who had the matter in charge, pointing to the grating on the rail as they came abreast of it.

"It is a fair and easy place from which to step to heaven, sir, or to the other place as well," said the Irishman, smiling, as he stepped on the rail. "I pray you to tell your men to start me on my way with a quick pull and a swift run." Pascoe nodded in comprehension. This would be a case in which speed would be merciful.

A boatswain's mate now stepped up beside the prisoner, and bound his feet and hands with a lashing. A hangman's knot had been made by expert fingers in the rope leading from the yard-arm, and the running noose was quickly cast about O'Neill's neck.

"The collar of an ancient order, this," observed O'Neill, still smiling. "And now one last request, sir," he added, turning to the lieutenant.

"And that is?"

"Throw away that black cap, sir. Let me go with my eyes open." The lieutenant hesitated a moment. The whole ship's company was filled with admiration for the intrepid and gallant Irishman.

"Do it, for God's sake, Pascoe!" whispered Coventry, springing up alongside O'Neill and the sailor, who, to avoid him, stepped back and stood on the rail by the fore shrouds.

"What are you doing there, Major Coventry?" answered Pascoe.

"Nothing. I promised to stand by him to the last," replied Coventry. The officer hesitated a moment, and then threw the cap into the water.

"I thank you," said O'Neill, huskily. "How much time is there?"

"About two minutes, I think," said the lieutenant, nervously.

"You will run away with the fall at the first or last stroke of the bell?"

ALMOST THE END

"The last, sir."

"No more," said O'Neill to Coventry, turning his face in the direction of the shore. The deep voice of the white-robed priest alone broke the silence, —

"*'Thou knowest, Lord, the secrets of our hearts; shut not Thy merciful ears to our prayer; but spare us, Lord most holy, O God most mighty, O holy and merciful Saviour, Thou most worthy Judge eternal, suffer us not, at our last hour, for any pains of death, to fall from Thee.'*"

Out on the water a white-sailed little boat was speeding swiftly toward them. There was a woman in it. The eyes of love, even in the presence of death, are keen, perhaps even keener then than ever. It was Elizabeth Howard. O'Neill recognized her at once. Good heavens! Why had she come here? She would arrive in time to see him swinging lifeless from the yard-arm, — a hideous sight for any woman. He could not take his eyes from her.

"See!" he whispered to Coventry, "that boat yonder; she is there."

"My God!" said the officer. "What shall we do?"

"Nothing; 't is too late."

"She has something in her hand," cried Coventry. "What can it be?"

"Forward, there!" cried the captain, watch in hand. "Strike the bell five!"

The mellow tones of the first couplet of the ship's bell rang out in obedience to the command. The hour was come! It was his death signal, but

THE GRIP OF HONOR

O'Neill never turned his head from the approaching boat. The old quartermaster struck the bell deliberately, lingering over it reluctantly; a little shiver ran through the men.

"Stand by!" shouted the lieutenant, in a voice he strove in vain to make firm. "Make a quick jerk and a lively run, lads, for God's sake!"

The men grasped the rope more firmly, sprang into position for the jump. The next couplet was struck on the bell. The boat was nearer now. Coventry saw that the woman waved something that looked like a paper in her hand. The last stroke of the bell rang out on the breathless, silent ship.

"Set taut!" cried the lieutenant, hoarsely. The men leaped forward instantly to the shrill piping of the boatswain and his mate. "Sway away!" he cried.

The tightened rope caught the Irishman by the throat. A lightning flash seemed to cleave the skies: he saw, as in a vision, a great hall hung with arras, a picture frame, a woman radiant, beautiful, her eyes shining; an upraised hand; like silver bells a voice murmured, "I love him, I love him." She moved — ah, a gigantic hand caught him by the throat; he strove to cry out; it clutched him tighter and tighter; blackness like a pall fell before him, shutting out the smiling face — death — agony — he saw no more — he swung into the air and was nothing.

The quick eye of Major Coventry had detected, at last, what the girl was waving.

ALMOST THE END

"That paper," he cried frantically, as the last bell struck. "It must be a reprieve; the admiral has relented."

Was it too late? Quick as thought he snatched the sheath knife from the belt of the sailor near him. It was too late to stop the men on the rope, even had he possessed the power; but as O'Neill rose in the air, he caught him around the waist, and with one rapid blow severed the straining rope above his head. Assisted at once by the sailor alongside of him, they lowered the bound, unconscious man upon the deck beneath them. It was all done in the twinkling of an eye. The men on the ship broke out in ringing cheers.

The rope, being relieved of the weight of the body, of course ran rapidly through the block, and the men hauling it pitched pell-mell over themselves upon the deck. There was a moment of intense excitement. The seamen on the other side of the deck, cheering wildly, started eagerly forward; the officers, sword in hand, sprang in front of them, driving them back. The marine officer aft brought his men at once to attention with a sharp word or two, and every piece was made ready in case of disturbance. Pearson, white with rage at the interruption, leaped forward.

"What is the meaning of this?" he shouted. "Who has dared to interfere in this manner?"

"I, sir," replied Coventry, fearlessly, looking up from his place by the unconscious man.

"And by what right, sir?" cried the enraged

captain. "Though you be the son of the admiral, you shall dearly rue this unwarranted assumption of authority. What excuse have you to offer for interrupting the sentence of a court-martial? What reason can you urge for your presumption?"

"Boat ahoy!" cried a seaman stationed at the port gangway.

"Sir," said Coventry, quietly meeting the eye of the thoroughly infuriated captain, "if I mistake not, you will find my excuse in that boat."

"Well for you, sir, if it be there! Never, in my twenty years of service, have I been so braved, and on my own ship, too. See what boat it is," said the captain, turning to one of his midshipmen, "and find out what is wanted." The lad came running back presently, and saluted.

"'T is a lady, sir, — the governor's ward, — Lady Elizabeth Howard; she wishes to come on board," he said.

"Lady Elizabeth Howard! This is no place for women; this man is still to be hanged. What can she wish?" exclaimed the captain, frowning.

"Receive her at once, sir, I beg," said Coventry. "She has a paper, — my excuse, sir," he added, smiling.

"Show her on board," said the captain, shortly, to the midshipman. Then he looked down on the still, unconscious form of O'Neill. "Send a surgeon here at once, sir," he continued; and as the latter presented himself, "Is the man dead?" he asked.

ALMOST THE END

"No, sir," said the surgeon, examining him hastily, and making ready to apply some necessary restoratives, for which he despatched an assistant to the sick-bay.

"Get him in shape, then, and quickly, for another attempt; for hang he shall, if he has to be held up for it," ordered the captain, sternly.

At this moment the midshipman, followed by Lady Elizabeth, pale as death, a blue boat cloak, which belonged to her guardian, which she had caught up in the castle, fluttering in the breeze, her hat gone, her hair dishevelled, her hand clutching a paper, broke through the little group.

"Captain Pearson, where is he?" she cried nervously; then, as her eyes fell on the prostrate form of O'Neill, she dropped the paper to the deck, covered her face with her hands, and rocked to and fro in agony. "Oh, my love, my love! Too late! too late!" she wailed, faltering.

"Not so, madam," said the captain, turning toward her. "The man still lives, the surgeon assures me. He has but fainted. Have you a warrant to stop the execution? If not, it must go on, and it shall go hard with Major Coventry as well."

"The prisoner is reprieved, sir; here is the paper," said Elizabeth, life coming back to her, "sealed and signed by the admiral himself. Oh, I had it a moment since — where has it gone?"

"Here it is, your Ladyship," said one of the officers, lifting it from the deck and handing it to her.

THE GRIP OF HONOR

"There!" she said, presenting it to the captain. He opened it deliberately and glanced over the brief contents. She watched him with a nervousness she vainly attempted to conceal. Meanwhile the doctor had succeeded in rousing O'Neill. The first glance of his eye fell on Elizabeth, and nothing else he saw.

"Heaven and the angels!" he murmured faintly, not yet comprehending the position.

"It seems to be made out properly and duly signed and sealed," said the captain, slowly, — "a reprieve for the prisoner until further notice, and permission for the bearer to see him alone," he added suspiciously. There was a little pause. He turned the paper over in his hand, and looked sharply at the girl.

"The admiral chooses a strange messenger," he added. "I cannot say if this be regular or no. His handwriting is unfamiliar to me. I do not recognize this; you say you had it from him, madam?"

Elizabeth could not trust herself to speak; she only bowed. There was evidently something very suspicious to the captain in the whole proceeding. The signature did not seem just right.

"Ah! I have it — Major Coventry!" he cried suddenly.

That miserable young man, sick at heart, had shrunk into the background since Elizabeth had come aboard, and the girl had not seen him before. He had felt that his work was done when she appeared; but, no, he was to find out that his troubles had but just begun.

ALMOST THE END

"Oh!" she cried, as he stepped forward, clutching him wildly by the arm, a look of terror in her eyes, as she added, in a whisper, "not you — I had forgotten you — we are lost!" In the bitter knowledge that she had forgotten him, he overlooked the clue to her action furnished by her last words.

"Here is a reprieve from the admiral," said the captain. "It seems to be correct, and yet — will you look over it and give me your opinion? you are familiar with his writing, at any rate. My Lady, forgive the questioning, but the matter is most serious, and I must be absolutely assured."

"Here is the paper, Edward," said Elizabeth, desperately, taking it from the captain's outstretched hand. "Is not that the writing of the admiral?" she added entreatingly, and then clasping her hands, she looked at him with all her soul in her eyes and waited, full of apprehension. A word, and he hanged her lover, and incidentally, but surely, killed her; a word, and he set them free! What the consequences to himself of his decision might be, with the sublime egotism of love for another, she neither knew nor questioned. Coventry gave a brief glance at the document; he saw what was expected of him; his life or her happiness trembled in the balance; true to his determination, he did not hesitate a moment. In that glance of a single second he realized the truth, which he had more than suspected before.

"It is," he replied briefly and indifferently aloud. A little prayer to God for forgiveness leaped within

THE GRIP OF HONOR

his heart at the falsehood. He had connived at her deceit, failed in his soldierly duty, broken his honor — for this woman. The reputation of a lifetime of loyal service to his king, the honorable record of years of devotion to duty had been thrown away in a moment for her. He had sacrificed more than life itself for his love — and she loved another! He turned the paper over in his hand and then quietly returned it to the captain. He said no other word, he scarcely even looked at Elizabeth. He could not trust his own gaze. There might be reproach in it. And he would fain make the sacrifice like a gentleman at least.

"Thank God — thank God — " whispered Elizabeth, under her breath; and the look of gratitude she flashed at him would have gone far to repay even a greater sacrifice — perhaps.

The keen captain was not yet satisfied, however.

"You wished to release him yourself, I remember," he said uncertainly. "I am by no means persuaded that — but it is impossible for me to proceed now until I have seen the admiral. Take the prisoner below," he said to the guard, "and allow Lady Elizabeth to see him alone. Mr. Pascoe, tell the boatswain to pipe down, and call the watch."

CHAPTER XV

A Soldier and a Gentleman

ACCOMPANIED by the marine guard, and leaning upon the arms of the surgeon and Coventry, who tenderly assisted his faltering steps, O'Neill was taken below, followed by Elizabeth, scarcely yet comprehending what had happened. The girl's heart was exulting madly. So far she had triumphed. What next? When they reached the little screened enclosure between the guns, in which O'Neill had been confined, the guard saluted and released the prisoner. He had not been ironed again, and by some oversight no one, in the confusion following the reprieve, called attention to it. As he stepped within the screen, and Elizabeth prepared to follow him, Coventry interrupted her by holding out his hand with a mute glance. Was she going to pass him by without a single word of gratitude, of farewell even?

"Oh!" she said, with unconscious cruelty which pierced his heart, for this was the second time, "I forgot you." And then, as if repenting for the situation, and to make amends for that forgetfulness, which was, to say the least, most ungrateful, in spite of the presence of the seamen and marines, she seized his hand, drew him toward her, and pressed a long, sweet kiss upon his forehead.

"God bless you for what you did," she whispered.

"What you do, do quickly," he replied. "I will replace the sentry; you will be safe. God grant you may succeed. 'T was bravely done; good-bye."

"Good-bye; we shall not forget you," she said hurriedly, withdrawing within the screen. And this was the only reward he received for his sacrifice. By his direction the sentry on guard withdrew to the opposite side of the deck, and he himself mounted guard in front of the canvas. With what feelings he paced to and fro in front of that little strip of cloth which alone separated him from the woman he loved, in the arms of the man who loved her — and he had put her there!

As soon as she entered the enclosure, Elizabeth threw herself in the arms of the bewildered O'Neill.

"Oh!" she whispered, "you are saved — saved — and through me!"

"No, dearest, not yet," replied he, straining her to his heart and kissing her fondly. "I scarcely yet understand it all; but if I heard aright, 't is but a reprieve until to-morrow; build no hope upon it."

"We will not wait for the morrow, my dearest," she answered softly, "for the boat swings under the counter yonder. When night falls and it is quite dark, we will slip out of the port and go away together; in a few moments it will be time."

The Irishman caught eagerly at the suggested idea. It was full of improbability, but it did pre-

A SOLDIER AND A GENTLEMAN

sent a bare possibility of escape if they were fortunate.

"Very good," he whispered, "excellent; but the sentry there?"

"We will wait until there is some bustle on the deck," she answered, "and in the confusion and noise they will not hear; at any rate, we must risk it." Something told her she would better not inform him that Coventry was keeping watch.

"How did you prevail upon the admiral to grant the reprieve?" he asked, after another pause, not unemployed, however.

"I — well, you see — oh, I scarcely know how; the admiral loves me, you know — I cannot explain it. It seems like a bewildering, frightful dream to me," said the girl, passing her hand over her hair and turning a shade paler as she spoke, and studiously avoiding his eye. "Do not speak of it now. You are safe for the moment — you saw the paper — Edward also — it was all right. Let that suffice."

He soothed her with tender words and loving caresses; the sound of them was death to the pale-faced young man, alone with his own broken thoughts on the other side of the screen. Unheeded the night came stealing over the harbor, lights in the town twinkled here and there, the boatswain's whistle rang out between decks on the frigate. There was a call, a hoarse cry or two, a hurrying of feet, a little confusion.

"Now is the time," said Elizabèth, releasing herself from his unwilling arms, and looking out through the port. "The man is watching; I met him on the strand as I was seeking for a boat to bring me out to you. He is faithful; he says he knows you — has served under you."

"Knows me!" said O'Neill, surprised, thrusting his head through the open port. There, right beneath him, a little skiff was being brought up deftly and without noise, from where it had lain unnoticed under the counter, in the confusion since the girl's arrival. The side of the ship was in deep shadow, and the broad main chains extending over their heads, above the ports, further concealed them from notice.

Gathering her skirts about her, Elizabeth slipped first through the port. O'Neill held her firmly until the man below lifted her gently into the stern of the boat. Noiselessly, and as quickly as possible, O'Neill followed her. By Elizabeth's direction, he lay down in the bottom of the boat, and she covered him entirely with her boat cloak. The man in the bows, whom O'Neill had not recognized in the shadow, and who had said nothing, slowly worked the boat back under the counter again; then, with a strong thrust, shoved her clear of the ship. The flooding tide carried them slowly away. In a few moments he cautiously got out his oars, and by a very gentle pulling added a little to the way of the boat.

The ear of the watchful Coventry had at once apprised him of their departure. He could scarcely resist the temptation to enter the screen, — to call

A SOLDIER AND A GENTLEMAN

them back that he might see her once again. But he had duty to do. So soon as he was persuaded that they had left the ship, he called the sentry from the opposite side of the deck, and told him to mount guard again, and on no account to disturb the prisoners. Then he ran rapidly up to the quarter-deck, and made his way aft to the marine on guard there. The man was looking out into the darkness at a dark blur on the water, — a boat; two figures could be distinguished in it, one of them a woman; Coventry saw them at once, and as he looked they disappeared, — the last sight of her, he thought bitterly. The marine had just opened his mouth to give the alarm, when the clear voice of the officer rang in his ear.

"Sentry!" said Coventry. The man instinctively sprang to attention at once, and for the moment forgot the boat.

"Have you seen any signals from the castle?"

"No, sir; but I seen a little boat off there that looked suspicious like."

"Whereabouts did you see it?"

"There, sir, right off there."

"No," said Coventry, straining his eyes through the darkness. "There is no boat there. You have been mistaken, I think," he added indifferently, his gaze still fixed on the place where they had drifted away and disappeared. He knew what was coming, since they had gone. He must pay for it, so he leaned on the rail and waited. A few moments later, a large barge, full manned, darted out of the

THE GRIP OF HONOR

darkness, coming toward the ship. Coventry knew what it was, of course.

"Boat ahoy!" shouted the watchful sentry at the gangway.

"Flag," was the answer, as the admiral dashed alongside. Almost before the officer of the watch could reach the gangway the old man clambered to the deck.

"Good-evening, sir," he said, in response to the former's salutation. "Captain Pearson?"

"I have sent for him, my Lord," replied the officer, and the next moment the captain himself came bustling out of the darkness to do honor to the old admiral.

"Ah, Captain Pearson, good-evening."

"Good-evening to your Lordship."

"The prisoner I sent off — he has been duly executed, I presume?"

"Why, no, sir!" said the captain, alarmed at this confirmation of his suspicions. "We were about ready to carry out the sentence; the command to sway aloft had been given, in fact, when we received your reprieve."

"My reprieve!" said the admiral, in great surprise. "What mean you? I sent no reprieve."

"Sir, sir!" cried the astonished captain. "It was brought here by your ward, Lady Elizabeth Howard."

"Elizabeth! Good God!" cried the old man, starting violently. "Her maid said she was ill — she must have — did you inspect it carefully, sir?" he asked, checking himself.

A SOLDIER AND A GENTLEMAN

"Yes, my Lord. It seemed to be all right; but the whole proceeding was so irregular and unlike you that I called upon—"

"Where is the paper?" cried the admiral, interrupting impatiently.

"I have just sent to fetch it, sir."

They waited in silence, until a midshipman placed it in the hand of the admiral. Pascoe held a light while the old man seized it, scrutinized it eagerly, and handed it back to the captain.

"This," he said slowly, "is a forgery. You should have disregarded it, sir."

"'T was passed upon by your son and aide, Major Coventry, my Lord," replied the captain, shortly.

"How! Edward! Where is he?"

"Here, my Lord," said the young man, stepping forward, pale as death, and saluting.

"Did you examine this paper, sir?"

"I did, sir."

"You knew it was a forgery?"

"Yes, sir."

"And yet you declared it to be correct?"

"I did, sir."

"For what purpose?"

"Will you direct these others to retire out of hearing, Captain Pearson?" said Coventry, indicating the officer of the watch, the midshipman, and all of the others; and when his request had been complied with, he added: "'T was to save the honor of your ward, my Lord, to insure happiness to the woman I love more than life, to effect the escape of the man upon whom that happiness depended."

"Have you dared, sir," said the admiral, furious with rage, "to thus derange my plans and disregard my orders, to thwart me, to interfere between a duly constituted court and its prisoner?" He stamped his foot and looked fiercely at his son.

"Me as well," said the captain; "upon the deck of my own ship — to put this dishonor upon me."

"The prisoner!" cried the admiral, impetuously. "Have him brought on deck at once, Captain Pearson."

"But your ward, my Lord; she is with him," said the captain.

"Bring her too, then," the old man answered passionately.

"But the crew — the men — not before them all!" said Coventry, striving to gain time.

"Before Heaven itself the offence was given," said the admiral, losing all control over himself in his fury, "and the punishment shall have equal publicity." The midshipman who had hastened below now came running on deck in terror.

"There's no one there, my Lord; they've gone, escaped, sir!" he cried.

"Impossible!" exclaimed Pearson.

"Escaped!" said the admiral, turning to the captain. "Had you no sentry to watch them, sir?"

"Yes, my Lord, certainly," said Pearson.

"Let him be tried and shot forthwith, then, for gross neglect of duty in permitting — "

A SOLDIER AND A GENTLEMAN

"My Lord, the sentry is innocent," interrupted Coventry; "I replaced him; I alone am guilty."

"Worse and worse!. You knew they escaped, sir?" said the admiral.

"I did; 't was to prevent discovery I took his place," replied his son, bowing. Captain Pearson opened his mouth to speak, but his superior silenced him with a wave of his hand.

A bitter fight raged in the old man's bosom, but he saw his duty, and knew it must be done. There was a long and awful pause. When the admiral spoke again it was in an altered tone; he had regained his self-control.

"Captain Pearson," he said slowly and deliberately, in a strained and unnatural voice, "let the court-martial which passed judgment upon the prisoner be re-convened at once to try Major Edward Coventry for disobedience of orders in time of war, and for aiding and abetting the escape of an enemy, and for knowingly declaring a forged order, purporting to bear my signature, to be correct, — in short, for conduct unbecoming an officer and a gentleman."

"Surely not that last, my Lord," said Coventry, impulsively raising his hand in deprecation.

The admiral hesitated, looked long and earnestly at his handsome son. "You may leave off the part about conduct unbecoming an officer and a gentleman, Pearson," he answered.

"Thank you, sir," said Coventry, gratefully.

"Good heavens, my Lord!" cried Pearson; "the punishment is death — I pray you — "

THE GRIP OF HONOR

"Silence, sir!" he cried sternly; "you have your order. Shall I be more merciful to this gentleman than to the poor marine I would have had shot a moment since for less than he has done?"

"But he is your son. Have mercy on him, my Lord!"

"So much the more imperative that he should receive justice — not mercy from me. Besides, from this hour he is no longer son of mine," said the old man, inflexibly. "Let the prisoner be confined under double guard; you will see that he at least does not escape you."

"It is just," said Coventry, no less resolutely than his father; "I expected it. It was for her I did it."

There was a sudden bustle upon the deck forward.

"Sail ho! Light ho! Light ho!" rang out from a dozen rough throats.

"Where away?" said the officer of the watch.

"Off the starboard quarter," was the reply, — "there, coming up from Flamborough Head."

"They will be the Bon Homme Richard and the rest of that scoundrelly pirate squadron, Captain Pearson. I saw them off Bridlington Bay this afternoon," said the admiral.

"We will go out and meet them at once, with your permission, my Lord," cried the captain, enthusiastically. "All hands up anchor! Mr. Pascoe, show the signal for the Scarborough to get under way. Lively! we have him now, men! This is our

A SOLDIER AND A GENTLEMAN

chance at last! There's prize money and honor for you by yonder lights!"

With wild cheers the eager crew broke for their stations. The capstan bars were shipped and manned, and the clanking pawls clicked merrily as the men heaved away as lustily as a crew homeward bound from a foreign station.

"Good luck to you, Captain Pearson," said the admiral, turning away. "Bring him back a prisoner or sink him, and I will pledge you my word your king's sword shall be laid upon your shoulders. Would that I were younger and might go with you! but my duties, as well, prevent me. Good-bye."

"Sir — my Lord — my father!" said Coventry, who had stood unnoticed in the excitement of the moment.

"Do I see you still here, sir?" answered the admiral, coldly.

"I would ask a favor of you, sir — as — as — as my father."

"Ask no favors of a father, sir; you have none!"

"Let me beg of the man, then," said Coventry, resolutely. "We are about to engage the enemy. For God's sake, sir, for the love of my mother, do not condemn me to inaction now! Let me serve as the humblest volunteer! You shall not regret it."

The old man hesitated. He was a father in spite of what he had said, and he could not forget it. His heart was throbbing beneath his iron exterior and appearance of outward composure.

"Go!" he replied at last. "You are free of any charges until to-morrow. When next I see you I shall have to prefer them, therefore let me not look upon your face again, sir. Do you understand?"

"Yes, yes; good-bye, sir!" said the young man, brokenly. "I thank you and bless you for this. To-morrow I shall plead my cause in a higher court. Think of me kindly, sir."

"And you have done this work and wrecked yourself for a woman! You have been a fool, sir; what woman that ever lived was worth it?" said the admiral, shortly.

"This one," replied his son. "I loved her; I love her still."

The two men looked at each other in silence. The admiral relented a little, — it was for the last time, — and drew the boy to him. He lifted his head to the sky in silent prayer.

"All hands make sail!" hoarsely cried the boatswain at the instance of the executive officer. "Lay aloft, topman!"

The admiral turned away, and Coventry was alone. He walked over to Captain Pearson.

"Father gives me a chance to die," he said. "Please assign me to some duty."

"I am glad to hear it," said the captain, his face lighting up. "We are short a lieutenant; I confide to you the forward division of the main-deck battery. Do your best with it."

"I hope to serve it well," said the young officer, saluting proudly, and springing toward his station.

A SOLDIER AND A GENTLEMAN

"Anchor's away, sir!" cried the officer forward on the forecastle.

"Man the topsail sheets and halliards, let fall, sheet home, hoist away!" roared the captain, himself seizing the trumpet. As the broad folds of canvas dropped from the wide-reaching yard-arms, the noble ship gathered way and sailed out to try her fortune.

BOOK IV

THE SELFISHNESS OF LOVE

BOOK IV

THE SELFISHNESS OF LOVE

CHAPTER XVI

In the Line of his Duty

AS soon as they had drifted some little distance from the Serapis, O'Neill rose, threw off the boat cloak, and stepped aft around the oarsman to the stern-sheets of the boat, where Elizabeth sat motionless, holding the tiller. He knelt down before her.

"Elizabeth, dearest, we have actually escaped!" he said softly, stooping toward her. "I did not think it possible." She released the tiller, took his head in her hands, and kissed him in wild exultation.

"Free! Free!" she murmured, "and together — my own, my own!" Her words, her look, her caress, set his blood bounding again.

"Yes, yes; is it not heavenly, and with you. Oh, my soul, how can I repay you?" he whispered, giving back kiss for kiss, and stretching out his hands toward her. There was a little pause, broken by a rough voice, which its owner evidently tried to render more gentle; in a hoarse whisper the man at the oars asked, —

"Where are ye a-headin' of the boat, yer Leddyship?"

THE GRIP OF HONOR

"I know not!" she answered wildly, seizing the tiller again; "only away from that awful ship!"

"Who is this man at the oars?" asked her lover, rising and sitting down by her when he took the tiller from her nervous hands.

"Well, yer Honor," said a low, deep voice, with a smothered laugh in it, "my name ashore, w'ere I was left by Cap'n Jones t'other night to look arter you, mought be Smith, or Brown, or any old name; but yere in this boat it's Price — William P. Price — w'ich is wot my mother told me, at any rate, though I ain't got no evidence but her word fur it, an' she's dead, an' God be thanked I see yer Honor alive."

"Price! You!" exclaimed O'Neill, in great surprise. "How did you find him, dearest?"

"I found her, please yer Honor," replied the man. "I seed her Leddyship a-comin' down to the beach, an' I ups and captures a small boat from the English, w'ich the man 'll be awful disappointed like, w'en he don't find her to-morrow, an' then I ups and offers to take her off, an' I tells her I knows you, an' we fixed it up, and here y' are!"

They were not yet so far from the Serapis, even by this time, but that the quick ear of the girl detected the confusion on her decks: the shrill piping of the boatswain and his mates, the sharp commands of the officers, the trampling of many feet, were easily heard; she clutched her lover nervously, all alert at the thought of a possible further danger to him.

IN THE LINE OF HIS DUTY

"Oh!" she whispered, "they are doing something on the ship. Our escape is discovered. They will come after us!"

"Not with the whole ship," he answered, smiling, though listening with straining apprehension as well.

"I think they're a-gittin' under way, sir," said the old seaman. "Listen to the clankin' o' the pawls, yer Honor."

"You are right; it cannot be after us, though; a cutter or two would suffice for that."

"It'll be fur the Richard an' the rest of 'em. Cap'n Jones, he said he'd capture them ships afore the mornin' watch, an' if you wasn't hung afore that time, he'd trice up the whole d—n—w'ich I beg pardon, yer Leddyship, but he said it—crowd to the yard-arms, unless they'd let you go free! Our wessels ought to be a-comin' up from Flamburry putty soon, now. But if I mought make so bold, w'ere are ye headin' fur now, sir?"

"We head for the Richard, of course," said the young man, promptly.

"That's w'ere we b'long," said the sailor, joyfully; "I don't want no fightin' goin' on, an' I ain't there!"

"Nor I," replied O'Neill. "I would put you ashore, Elizabeth, before we go; but—"

"'Whither thou goest, I will go; thy people shall be my people,'" she quoted softly. "Whom have I now but you? To whom can I go but to you?" she murmured, laying her hand upon his own. It was dark on the boat, but if it had been broad daylight he could not have helped it, — he kissed her.

"Oh, to be worthy of it all, to be worthy!" he answered.

William grinned sympathetically, wiped his mouth wistfully with the back of his hand, and tried to look away. Presently, unshipping the oars, the two men stepped the mast and hoisted the small sail. The little boat, under the freshening breeze, began to draw through the water rapidly. In order to win out of the mouth of the harbor, they would have to pass in a direction which would bring them once more near the moving Serapis. They could hardly hope to escape discovery. They had, of course, gained a good start on the frigate; but as she was soon covered with sails, and her great height enabled her to catch the freshening breeze blowing over the hills, which was lost to the smaller craft, she literally rushed down upon them.

A noble picture she made to those on the boat. Ghostlike and eerie in the pale moonlight, shining fitfully through the overcast heavens, the great white ship towered above them, her soaring masts covered with clouds of snowy canvas stretching far out on either side on the spreading yard-arms. Her sails swept the skies; her keel ploughed the deeps; the wind sang in the top-hamper; the white water, shot with sparks, piled up in front of her, bubbled and played around her forefoot, and rolled away on either side in broad sheets of foamy phosphorescence.

IN THE LINE OF HIS DUTY

The yellow lights of the battle lanterns streamed through her open ports; a drum was grimly rolling the call to battle on her decks. Dark forms passed to and fro; men leaped hither and thither in casting loose the double row of great black guns; sometimes a vivid flash in the moonlight proclaimed a drawn sword. Presently the cries and orders died away; the men settled down at their stations; silently the huge fabric, a splendid example of that power which for twice two hundred years had ruled the seas, swept toward them. O'Neill watched her in generous admiration.

"A fit antagonist even for our great captain," he cried, all his enthusiasm aroused by the ship, "and nobly handled," he added. "Mark the discipline; see the order!"

"Ay, sir, that'll be a hard one to take; but we'll take her, never fear!" said the old seaman, sharing his officer's ungrudging approbation of their gallant foe.

"How can you speak so?" said the girl. "To me she is nothing but a prison — a menace — a horror!"

"You are a woman, dearest; I hope to be on the old Richard before long, and I feel from such a ship as that there is much honor to be gained."

"And death, too," she answered, shuddering.

"It may be; death and honor often go hand in hand," he replied gravely; "but she nears us; you must lie down until she passes."

It was a new thing for her to be commanded; she

found it altogether a sweet experience — then. Later it might be another matter. So, though protesting because she was a woman and had prescient eye to the future, Elizabeth dutifully obeyed her lord and lay down in the boat, resting her head against his foot. As they drew toward the mouth of the harbor the wind came stronger. The little boat fairly roared through the white-capped waves. She heeled over until the water trickled in on the lee side; but O'Neill resolutely and skilfully held her up to it. He could not afford to lose an inch of distance to leeward, for the water shallowed rapidly in that direction, and abounded in rocks as well. The Serapis was alongside now; they had not yet been observed. The attention of the men on the frigate was fixed upon the approaching ships to the southeast, now plainly visible. O'Neill fairly held his breath as he congratulated himself that they were to be passed by unnoticed. Suddenly a sharp cry rang out just as the Serapis drew ahead.

"Sail ho! Boat ahoy, there!" For a moment the small boat lay right in the path of light cast by the brilliantly illuminated stern-ports of the frigate.

"'T is the prisoner, he that escaped!" shouted a powerful voice.

"Sentry, give him a shot from your piece," cried Captain Pearson himself, springing on the rail and leaning over toward them. Old Price shook his fist at the frigate in stout defiance. The sharp crack of a musket rang out in the air. The bullet seemed to have struck something forward in the boat; a

The sharp crack of a musket rang out in the air.

IN THE LINE OF HIS DUTY

shudder swept through the little craft, a hoarse, frightful cry quivered through the night, there was a splash, the boat struck something, and that something, whatever it was, rasped along her keel as she drove ahead.

"Clear away the second cutter," cried another voice on the frigate.

"Keep all fast!" shouted Pearson. "We have bigger game to-night," and then he hollowed his hand and cried out as the Serapis drew rapidly away, —

"We'll take care of you, sir, in the morning, when we return." A few more musket-shots were fired at them from different parts of the ship; one bullet tore through the sail and whistled by the ear of the young lieutenant, but did no harm.

"We are saved again!" cried Elizabeth, sitting up and looking gratefully at her lover.

"But not without a cost," said the young man, solemnly.

"What mean you? Are you hurt; are you wounded?" she cried.

"Price!" called O'Neill, softly, though he knew it was useless. There was no answer.

"Oh, that awful cry!" said Elizabeth, shuddering.

"It was he," added O'Neill, gravely. "He was hit by the first shot, and went overboard. Did you not feel him strike the keel?"

"Is there no hope for him?" she queried anxiously. "Could we not put back and seek him?"

"None," replied the young lieutenant, shortly.

THE GRIP OF HONOR

"There was death in his voice; it's all over with him. Well, he died in the line of his duty; 'tis a sailor's cherished hope."

"He helped me — both of us — in time of need; our way to liberty and happiness," she cried piteously, "seems to be over the bodies of those who love us."

"So it has ever been in the world, — a thousand deaths to make one life, a thousand griefs to make one joy," he answered, laying his hand tenderly upon her head, which she had buried in her hands.

"But what come what may," she added, looking up resolutely, with all the selfishness of love, "I have you, at least, and we are together again."

"Ay, let us pray it may be forever, sweetheart."

They were out of the harbor now; and while the Serapis was stretching along to the northeast to gain an offing, with the Scarborough some distance ahead of her, and to leeward, the lighter draft of the small boat permitted O'Neill to head her directly for the oncoming American ships, whose lights, and the ships themselves, were now plainly visible in the moonlight.

CHAPTER XVII

Differing Standards

"THE battle which will take place to-night yonder between those ships decides my fate. I hope to God I may arrive in time to take my part in it! The Richard is fearfully short of officers at best; Landais, who has the Alliance, is crazy and a coward; Cottineau in the Pallas is an unknown quantity, and the rest have fled. Jones has only Richard Dale and a lot of midshipmen with him upon whom he can absolutely depend, and there are over two hundred prisoners in the hold. He needs me. If this breeze hold on, I think we may intercept the Richard before the battle is joined. Pray, dearest, as never before, for the success of our arms! It means life, and you, for me."

"It means life for me as well," she answered, nestling against him and nerving herself up to the inevitable confession. How he would take it she did not know, or rather she would not permit herself to say. She was conscious only of an impelling necessity to tell him the whole story, though she had deliberately waited until she believed he could do nothing.

"Ah, yes, 't is sweet of you to say so, but not the same. Me they will hang, but not you," he answered fondly.

"Yes, they will," she replied. "I — I — I must confess it to you before we go further; it weighs upon me. I also am guilty."

"Guilty! You! Of what, pray? Of loving me too much?" he queried, laughing in pure lightness of heart.

"No, not that," she answered, "but that — that order — your reprieve. It was — the admiral did not sign it," she added desperately.

The secret was out.

"And who did it, then?" he asked, still unsuspicious of her meaning.

"I did it myself," she answered, with averted head.

"It is not possible!" he exclaimed, withdrawing from her a little in his astonishment.

"'T was for you — for you I did it — reproach me not; nay, you shall not!" she cried, on fire to defend herself and her love, now the truth was told. "Captain Jones said six hours' delay and you were saved. There was no other way. I begged, implored, entreated the admiral — he left me; went away — I saw the man fixing that block — the rope — I ran to him to make one more appeal — he was not there. On his desk was an order giving me permission to see you, which he had intended to give me and had refused at the last moment and left unsigned. His watch was there and his seal. I added the rest and signed and sealed it myself; do not shrink from me!" she pleaded with changed mood again. "Your anger — your disapproval — kills me. Is there no excuse that you can find for me?" Her

DIFFERING STANDARDS

appeal was so tender, her affection so apparent, she was her own justification.

"No man would have done it," he said irresolutely, wavering.

"But every woman would," she replied promptly, pressing her advantage. "Why are you so silent; Your precious honor is safe, and as for mine —"

"'T was nobly done," he answered at last, in complete surrender. "There is not a woman in the world but would honor you for it; not a man who would not love you. You have done that which I could not, and for me. My heart before, and now my life is yours, my heart's dearest."

"I knew you would not like it," she answered simply, "but there was no other way. I confess I was terrified when Edward —"

"Good heavens!" cried O'Neill. "He saw the order?"

"Yes," said the girl, cowering before him again. In truth, this phase of the transaction had actually escaped her memory.

"Captain Pearson accepted it without questioning him?" he queried. She would have given all the world to lie to him, but even in the darkness she could not be further untrue, in his very presence, though now like a flash she saw it all.

"He — he doubted it," she whispered hesitatingly. "He handed the paper to Edward, and asked him if it — if it was all right."

"And Coventry?"

"He took it and looked at it, looked at me —

THE GRIP OF HONOR

I had forgotten him, I must confess, — " she went on brokenly, — " and then he handed it back to Captain Pearson and — and said it was correct — the signature, I mean."

"He knew, think you?" asked her lover, with deadly calmness.

"Yes, he knew," she faltered.

"And the sentry — our unheeded escape?"

"Edward took his place — I might as well tell you all now," continued the girl, desperately.

"Ah!" he said, coldly and sternly; "and do you know, Lady Elizabeth, what the penalty is for such actions as his?"

"No," she replied, in alarm; "I never thought. They will not harm him. He is the son of the admiral — what is it?"

"They will shoot him, or hang him like a dog to the very yard-arm prepared for me!" he answered with stern emphasis.

"No, no! It is not possible!" she cried, appalled at the naked fact.

"Ay, but it is," he replied; "and it is through your actions, and my blind acquiescence therein, that this honorable gentleman is done to death. This puts another face on the whole thing. You have made me a craven; I am dishonored, his life is sacrificed for me!"

"I did not mean to do it; I did not know," she wailed, stricken to the heart by his bitter reproach.

"Ay, but you should have known; but when women meddle in affairs of state the consequences

DIFFERING STANDARDS

oft exceed their narrow views. Pray God, there may yet be time to rectify the frightful happening," said O'Neill, bitterly, putting the helm hard over as he spoke. The boat swept around, the sail gybed, and they headed for the northeast.

"What is it that you would do?" cried Elizabeth, in alarm, laying her hand on the tiller.

"Follow the Serapis," he answered shortly.

"For what?"

"To give myself up if possible, and thus insure his freedom."

"I knew — I knew it would be so," she whispered. "I loved him," she murmured, turning away, "I have sacrificed everything for him, and he repudiates, reproaches me. O my God, why hast thou forsaken me!" she wailed in unconscious imitation of a greater Sufferer. She drew away from him and knelt down in the boat, and buried her face in her hands, leaning upon the weather gunwale. He looked at her a moment, and before the pathetic abandonment of her grief his anger melted. She was a woman; with her, love was all.

"Elizabeth," he said tenderly, "the bitterness of having caused that good man's death, his apparent dishonor, overwhelmed me. I love you, as you know, more than life itself. You are a woman; you see things differently. There is nothing above love in a woman's heart. Come back to me; your place is here, whatever happens. I love you the more for your great sacrifice, but now we must undo it if we can. Heaven has not smiled upon our meeting;

perhaps, if we go hand in hand before God together, we may find mercy, perhaps joy!"

She made no answer, but nestled against him forgiven, contented. For a time they sailed the sea in silence. The clouds had broken and left a clear sky, whence the moon had flooded the ocean with her silvery light; but the breeze came fitfully and gradually died away where they were now under the lee of the land. It was such a night as lovers dream of. They loved and they were together, side by side, alone, in the soft autumnal night, adrift on a summer sea. There was that in the past which kept them silent; and yet in their very proximity, in the hands that touched and clasped each other, the head that nestled on his shoulder, the arm that encircled her waist, the lips that met, the eyes that spoke, — there was a sweetness which neither had ever known before. The gentle wind whispered of love. The curling, lipping waves caressed the keel with sounds like kisses, and to it all their hearts kept time. It was a respite, — a lull between two phases of the conflict; there was love and there was peace in the little boat, and war and tumult were far off on the horizon.

By and by Elizabeth slipped down from the thwart, and crouched down in the boat at his feet. O'Neill held the tiller with one hand; the other lightly stroked her golden head. She was perfectly content; everything was out of her heart but he and the present; she was very still. He could see the soft curve of her cheek resting upon her sweet white hand in the

DIFFERING STANDARDS

moonlight. After one of the little intervals of silence, he looked down upon her again. She made no motion, and did not reply to a word he said softly, and he discovered that she was asleep.

He did not wonder. The experiences of the past few days would have killed any ordinary woman. How heroic she had been! With what abandon she had put aside everything for the purpose of saving him! She had hesitated at nothing. His love for her was measured by his honor; hers for him was boundless. 'Twas ever so; and he had reproached her, spoken harshly to her, upbraided her, turned away from her! How could he have been so cruel! she was so young, his heart yearned over her. He vowed that if God did permit them to escape from the perils which environed them, he would make up to her for every unkind word spoken, every reproach, every cutting glance, by an eternity of devotion.

The night, the ocean, the loneliness, impressed him. What had he ever done to be so blessed in the love of this noble woman? His life, as he had said, had been an idle one. In the courts he had played at hearts as he had played at war on the ships for the fun of the game. With her a serious purpose had entered his life and was before him. The silence of the night was broken only by the soft splash of the waves, as the little boat rocked gently through them. The gentle wind grew fainter and fainter; presently the flap of the idle sail against the mast apprised him that it had gone.

The white Serapis and her consort were far, far

ahead, going fast and leaving a long white wake across the sea. They seemed to have kept the breeze which had failed the small boat. Coming up from the southward he could see the black shapes of the Richard and her attendant ships. What would he have given to be upon the deck by the side of that dauntless captain! But even could he approach the two ships, that privilege would be denied him, for honor demanded that he present himself upon the deck of the Serapis without delay. It might be that it would be too late even then to save Coventry, but he would go and do his best. When the boat lost way, he sat a moment in indecision. He was so loath to awaken the tired girl, but it was necessary. Gently he raised her head.

"Why, my dearest," she said, "was I asleep? What has happened? Oh!" it came back to her, "you are going back to the Serapis." Then she looked eagerly forward. The ships were far off now, several miles away; and as the breeze still held with them, the distance was increasing with every passing moment.

"We do not advance," she cried, a note of joy in her voice, as her ear detected the flapping of the sail; "the wind has died out. She laughed triumphantly, "We shall never reach them."

"And poor Coventry?" said O'Neill.

"I cannot help it," she answered simply. "I think only of you. Now if I could go back alone and take his place and let you go free, I would cheerfully do that."

DIFFERING STANDARDS

"What advantage would that be to me?" he asked her.

"Well, there is little use in our discussing it any more," she answered, "for you cannot reach either ship now before it is over. The wind has gone over to them, and we are still."

"Ah, but I have another way of getting along."

"How is that?"

"I shall row," he said quietly. "Will you take the tiller?"

"No!" she replied defiantly, folding her arms. "I will not help you at all!"

"Elizabeth! Elizabeth!" he murmured.

"I will not, I tell you!" she said. "Frankly, I do not wish to. What is Edward, what are those ships, what is the whole wide world to me beside your safety?"

"I must do it alone as best I can, then," said O'Neill, leaving her side and going forward and un-stepping the mast and thrusting out the oars, which he handled with the skill of long practice and strong arms. The difference of speed between the boat and the two ships was now of course greater than before.

"Why fatigue yourself unnecessarily?" she said to him at last, after he had been rowing for some time. "You gain nothing; 'tis useless."

"No matter," was his reply as he desperately tugged at the oars. "I shall at least have the consciousness of knowing I did what I could." But after pulling hard for an hour, he leaned over the handles of the oars and turning his head looked forward. She was right; it was a perfectly hopeless task. The nearest ships were now ten or a dozen miles away, and going farther, when a flash of light pierced the darkness on the horizon, followed some time after by the roar of a heavy gun.

BOOK V

IN THE HELL OF BATTLE, ALL

CHAPTER XVIII

The Boys in Command

"THE ship is clear, sir," said Lieutenant Richard Dale, saluting smartly. He was a handsome, dashing young sailor, the picture of sea gallantry, as he ran lightly up the ladder from the main-deck and stopped before the little captain of the Bon Homme Richard, standing on the weather side of the poop, keenly surveying the scene.

"Very good, sir," said the little man, nodding his head but not turning toward his executive officer. "Look yonder," he added, pointing ahead and toward the shore. "What do you make that, sir?"

"It cannot be the Alliance!" exclaimed Dale, in great surprise, as he shaded his eyes and gazed intently in the direction of the setting sun at a large war-ship which was edging in shore toward the harbor of Scarborough, which apparently sheltered a numerous convoy of merchant ships.

"'T is indeed she!" replied Jones, sternly; "I have repeatedly signalled to Captain Landais to follow in our wake,—to form line ahead. If we get out of this thing safely—" He stopped, repressed his feeling by a strong effort, compressing his lips passionately in a way which promised trouble for Captain Landais and the Alliance, a new and handsome frigate, the

THE GRIP OF HONOR

best of Jones's squadron. After a momentary pause the commodore, a man of few words in time of action at least, turned toward the stern of his ship.

"Look aft there, too," he added.

"That will be the Pallas, of course," said Dale, as his eye fell upon a smaller ship which was following the Bon Homme Richard. "And the Vengeance, sir?"

"There! Hull down on the horizon, fleeing like a coward," said Jones, bitterly.

"And those two white fellows forward there," continued Dale, "reaching out from the harbor —"

"Are the Serapis and the Scarborough," interrupted the captain, "if the information sent us by O'Neill be correct."

"Would he were here!" exclaimed Dale.

"Yes, he is himself a host," said Jones, sadly. "We are fearfully short-handed. O'Neill gone, and Henry and Cutting Lunt, our third and fourth officers, both absent. The Frenchmen are an unknown quantity. I have only you, Dale, and Stacey and Mease, and the boys, of course; but I can depend upon you."

"Upon me — upon all of us," replied Dale, gallantly, "to the death itself!"

"I know it," said the captain, smiling and laying his hand affectionately upon the young man's shoulder. "They are very young, though," he continued gravely, "for such desperate work as this promises to be, but they are brave hearts and true. They will do their best, I doubt not."

THE BOYS IN COMMAND

"With you to command them, sir, they'll not be found wanting, I am sure," said the enthusiastic Dale, who was devotedly attached to his great commander There was a little pause.

"Messieurs," said Jones, turning toward a little group of French officers who were standing on the lee side of the poop. At the captain's word they stepped forward and saluted gracefully.

"Colonel de Weibert, you have served in the artillery, I believe?" asked the captain of a fine-looking veteran. The Frenchman bowed. "Will you assist Lieutenant Dale in working the battery on the main-deck? It is an unusual place for a soldier, but we are very short of experienced officers. You understand the handling of great guns. It would be a great favor."

"Any place which enables him to fight the enemy is a good place for a soldier, my captain. I am at Lieutenant Dale's service," replied the gallant old soldier.

"You, vicomte, and gentlemen," said Jones, turning to De Chamillard, who was attended by several subalterns, "will take charge of the soldiers on the quarter-deck and forecastle. I desire a continuous small-arm fire to play upon the decks and tops of the English ships."

"Sir captain," smilingly answered De Chamillard, a dapper, dainty little man, as he in turn bowed profoundly, laying his hand on his sword, "not a man shall escape my marine infantry; I answer for them and for my friends here as well," he added

THE GRIP OF HONOR

indicating his gay-clad lieutenants, who emulated the vicomte in the profundity of their salutations.

"Remember, gentlemen," said Jones, his face lighting, "'t is for the honor of America — and of France. Mr. Brooks," he said to an alert young midshipman who was acting as his signal officer and aide, "signal the Pallas to edge off to the east and engage the smaller ship of the enemy. The big fellow is our game, messieurs. See! they are forming line ahead and are waiting for us. Brave fellows! Quartermaster," he cried, stepping to the break of the poop and looking down at the old seaman and his mates stationed at the wheel, "d' ye see those two ships?"

"Ay, ay, sir," answered the veteran tar, shading his eyes with his hand and peering eagerly ahead; "I sees 'em, yer Honor."

"That's well. The one ahead, nearest the shore, is our mark. I intend to round to on her port bow. Mind your course!"

"Very good, sir," answered the steersman, giving a knowing squint at the lifting sails, and shifting the wheel a few spokes.

"Now, gentlemen," continued the captain, "to your stations all! But stay — Mr. Brooks, direct the sailing-master, purser, and the junior officers to come up on the quarter-deck."

In a short time the two older officers and a little band of youths whose ages ranged from twelve to seventeen years stood before the captain and saluted. His eyes fell tenderly upon the boys; so youthful and immature were they to be charged with the

THE BOYS IN COMMAND

heavy responsibilities of the coming hour, which would have devolved upon the older men but for their unfortunate absence.

"Young gentlemen," he said quietly, "accident has thrust you into positions of great responsibility which otherwise you might not have been called upon to fill for years. We are about to engage two powerful ships of the enemy. The Richard is heavily overmatched in everything except in the spirit and courage of her officers and men. I am determined — nay, we are all determined, are we not? — that the flag which floats above us shall never be struck. We may be sunk, but we will not surrender. I shall try to do my part; you will, I doubt not, do yours?"

"Ay, ay, sir."

"We will, sir."

"Count on us to the death, sir," broke forth from the impetuous youths who clustered about the captain.

"Remember that we are fighting not only to uphold the honor of our flag in the face of the most arrogant navy on the ocean, but to rescue from a shameful death — if it be not unhappily too late — one of our brother officers who would give his life to be here."

"O'Neill, O'Neill!" cried one and another, the brave Irishman being a great favorite with all.

"I enjoin upon you the utmost vigilance and care. Supplement your inexperience by redoubled effort. Be as brave as youths and as cool as veterans. Give implicit obedience to the orders you receive from Mr. Dale, Mr. Stacey, or from me, and exact the same compliance with your orders from your men. They are a hard lot to handle; don't lose control of them." He paused a moment, scanning the intent faces of the lads close about him, and then continued: "Remember, too, we have more than one foe to fight, — the prisoners below, the enemies yonder on the sea, and disobedience in our own squadron. Who keeps guard over the prisoners in the hold?"

"I, sir, with the master-at-arms," answered Payne, a resolute-looking youth of fifteen. "I wanted to be on deck in the batteries, sir —"

"You could have no more important station, my lad," replied the captain. "Keep them under hatches! Do not hesitate to shoot the first man who makes a move to break out! They must not be allowed to gain the deck. At all hazards, keep them down! I repeat it, sir, keep them down! Do you understand?"

"Yes, sir," gravely answered the boy, awed by the emphasis of the captain's manner.

"You, Mr. Mayrant, with Mr. Mease the purser and Mr. Brooks, will remain on deck with Mr. Stacey and me," continued the captain. "You, Mr. McCollin, will take charge of the old eighteen-pounders on the berth-deck. You, too, have a post of danger! Be careful of them! I distrust them greatly, yet they must be tried."

"Ay, ay, sir. Thank you, sir," said the young midshipman, delighted at being thus distinguished.

THE BOYS IN COMMAND

"Mr. Caswell," he added, turning to the largest and oldest, "you will take charge of the forecastle. Mr. Fanning, I confide the maintop to you. The rest of you will command the several divisions in the main batteries and the other tops. Now, young gentlemen, before you go to your stations, I would take you by the hand; and so," lifting his cocked hat reverently, an example all present followed, "may God guard the right!" There was a suspicious moisture in some of the eyes looking upon the captain, but the midshipmen would have died rather than permit an actual tear to be seen.

"Three cheers for Commodore Jones and the bully Richard!" at last shouted Payne, breaking the insupportable silence. The little party, somewhat forgetful of discipline for the moment, crowded around their captain, shaking him by the hand, and turned away. They had come up to the quarter-deck a rollicking set of boys; they returned from it a group of grave-eyed men.

"What a splendid set of youngsters!" said Jones to himself, as he watched them spring lightly toward their stations. Then he turned toward the sailing-master: "Mr. Stacey, take the deck for a few moments and hold on as we are. Ah!" he said, pausing with his foot on the ladder as he saw the Pallas, a much swifter sailer than the Richard, rushing by on the starboard side with every breath of canvas drawing, heading for the smaller of the two English ships before them, "there goes the Pallas. Cottineau, at least, is a brave man. I shall remember him. Come, Dale." As he stepped down the ladder a hearty cheer rang out from the passing frigate, which, without order, was lustily returned from the Richard, and then the two officers walked through the batteries.

The sun had set for some time, and night had long since fallen over the sea. The light-house on Flamborough Head was sending out a great beam of warning from that jutting point. Far on the horizon a silvery brightness had spread itself in the heavens, bespeaking the harvest moon, the burnished rim of which even before sunset had leaped into being on the edge of the water. Lights twinkled here and there on the English ships before them and crowned the hills of the distant town and harbor. Battle lanterns were lighted between decks on the Richard, the yellow flickering radiance from which was reflected from the sinewy, half-naked, sweat-covered bodies of the stalwart men at their quarters, as the captain walked through the crew.

It was a varied assemblage of about three hundred men which manned the guns and filled the tops. The crew had been made up in France out of such materials as came to hand. There were about seventy-five tried and true American seamen, most of them veterans of many a hard fight and bold adventure. These commanded the different guns and filled the more important stations. There were, perhaps, one hundred and fifty veteran French soldiers, — old artillerists, — some of whom had volunteered at the guns; a few of the most expert marksmen among them were

THE BOYS IN COMMAND

stationed in the tops, but the greater portion was divided into two large bodies drawn up on the quarter-deck and forecastle. The balance of the crew had been gathered from the riff-raff of all nations; perhaps a tougher, rougher, harder, more desperate body of men never fought a ship; they had but one virtue,— they would fight.

Only a resolute hand and an indomitable will like that of Jones had ever held the motley crowd in any kind of discipline. He had ruled the Richard with an iron heart, and in spite of bitter murmurs had forced the men to do his will. The ship had been a slumbering volcano of incipient mutiny and latent rebellion; but in the presence of the enemy, these men whose passion it was to fight forgot their personal grievances, and mindful of the finished skill and superhuman courage of their captain, looked favorably upon him and eagerly anticipated the conflict. Rude jests and bits of sea pleasantry, usually permitted in moments like these, flew up and down the line between the captain and the ruffians under his command as he passed by them in rapid review.

The watches had been piped to supper earlier than usual, and afterward a double ration of grog had been served out. The men were in good spirits, and good spirits in them! The captain carefully examined every part of the ship. The young midshipmen who filled the unwonted stations, evidently deeply impressed by their opportunities and responsibilities, were pacing restlessly up and down, eagerly scrutinizing every detail of their several commands. On the berth-deck, standing before the hatch which led into the hold in which over two hundred English prisoners were confined, the commodore found young Payne, attended by the master-at-arms, two American seamen, and three French soldiers, keeping guard.

"Ah! I am glad to see you at your station," said the captain, raising his voice, as the young midshipman, full of pride, saluted him. "You remember my orders, sir, which were to shoot the first man who shows his head above the hatch?"

There was a hoarse murmur from the prisoners beneath the gratings which covered the hatchway, at this speech of the captain's, which was, as he had intended, clearly heard by them.

"Ay, ay, sir. I'll do it; never fear," answered the lad, in his boyish treble.

"Remember, sir, that I regard your station as one of the most important on the ship! Those men must not be allowed on deck!"

"They shall not be!" answered Payne, resolutely. "If the ship goes down, they go with it!"

There was a harsh roar below; oaths, curses, imprecations, and cries were blasted up from the deck beneath them.

"Silence there!" shouted Jones. "Remember!" he said to the midshipman as he turned away.

"I shall not forget, sir," replied the boy, saluting proudly.

"Do what you can," said Jones, turning to McCollin, — "do what you can with the old eighteens."

THE BOYS IN COMMAND

"They shall be fought as long as they exist, sir," answered the young officer.

"I know that, sir," said Jones, glancing approvingly from him to the little groups of half-naked men clustered about the guns, the sweat streaming from their muscular bodies in the heat of the narrow, confined quarters, "and you have the men with you who will back you up."

A hoarse cheer which resounded throughout the dim recesses of the berth-deck bespoke the hearty acquiescence of the men in their captain's shrewd estimate of their qualities.

CHAPTER XIX

'Tween Decks with the Men

THE captain, not ill pleased at this and other manifestations of hearty spirit which had met him on every hand, mounted the ladders and resumed his station on the high poop-deck of the frigate.

Anything less like a war vessel could hardly be imagined. The Bon Homme Richard had been an old-fashioned, high-pooped East Indiaman with a towering forecastle. This antiquated makeshift, formerly called the Duc de Duras, had been turned over to Jones for a ship-of-war through the grudging kindness of France. It was the best ship Franklin and the other commissioners of the new American Republic could procure for their greatest sea captain. Jones, out of compliment to Franklin, author of the "Poor Richard" papers, had renamed her; the name was the only thing new about her. She had been pierced for thirty-six guns, twenty-eight twelve-pounders on the main-deck, and eight nine-pounders on the quarter-deck and forecastle. In utter desperation at her entire inadequacy, Jones had recourse to the dangerous experiment, not often resorted to, of mounting six eighteen-pounders in ports pierced for them on the berth-deck, and of course very near the

'TWEEN DECKS WITH THE MEN

water line. The guns were all of an obsolete pattern and much worn by use, the eighteen-pounders being especially bad; as dangerous, in fact, to friends as foes. Bad as they were, they were all he could obtain, and, with characteristic determination, Jones resolved to make the best of them.

The ship herself was so old and rotten that she was not even fit for an ordinary merchant cruise, much less prepared for the shocks of battle. Through an unfortunate combination of circumstances, all of her senior officers were absent except Dale, the first lieutenant, Stacey, the sailing-master, and Mease, the purser. Among that half of her crew who were soldiers, many had scarcely yet acquired their "sea-legs," and some of them were actually sea-sick during the battle! The Serapis, with which they were about to engage and to which they were rapidly drawing near, was a brand-new, double-banked frigate, mounting fifty guns on two covered and one uncovered decks, twenty eighteen-pounders, twenty nines, and ten sixes. She was manned by three hundred and fifty well-drilled able seamen and commanded by one of the best officers in the English navy, who was ably seconded by a full quota of capable and experienced subordinates.

Pearson had no more doubt of winning the victory than he had of the rising of the sun next morning. Leaving one factor out of a comparison of the opposing forces, his confidence was absolutely warranted. But Jones had no more doubt of winning the victory than Pearson had. Pearson knew his ship and his crew;

Jones knew himself. He was the unconscious factor which vitiated Pearson's conclusions. When a man like the little Scotch-American captain makes up his mind to do a thing, there is only one thing to prevent his doing it, and that is to remove the man! Jones *intended* to conquer. There never was a man who had more of the spirit of absolute determination, of unconquerable, unshakable, unbreakable pertinacity in continuing a conflict, than he. He never knew when he was beaten; perhaps because he never was. There was something in the sheer determined, persistent pugnacity of the man which absolutely compelled success. He wrenched victory from overwhelming odds, superior force, fortuitous chance, — everything.

The men understood this, too. There is nothing your real hard-bitten dare-devil, your imprudent ruffian, likes so much as a man who is not afraid of him and who will be his master. Your ruffian curses and swears at your man, plots against him, rebels, mutinies, conspires, and in the moment of action follows him like a devotee. The little man standing at the break of the poop, cool, calm, thoughtful, with his student face and somewhat poetic, dreamy smile, did not look like the iron-handed, iron-willed, indomitable master of the motley ruffian band which had been dumped upon his deck — which he certainly was. With the dainty manner of a Frenchman, the courteous deference of a gentleman of the oldest and best school, the calmness of an ancient philosopher, there was in his appearance no outward

'TWEEN DECKS WITH THE MEN

evidence of the tremendous qualities inherent in the man, save in the sparkling, flashing, piercing eye which plunged through and through those upon whom its glances were fastened, with the keenness of a sword-blade.

His men were wont to say that he could *look* even a frigate into striking her colors if given an opportunity! The hardest ruffian cringed like a cur before him, and this when he was peaceful and quiet. When he grew angry, which was rare, his passion was like Washington's, blasting and appalling. He was perfectly quiet now, however, and he stood by Dale's side at the break of the poop looking over the bows of the ship toward the enemy.

As they swept forward through the peaceful sea, a fragrance of balm and spicery and myrrh, which seemed to suggest the many voyages of the old ship in the distant tropic latitudes, clung about the decks and pervaded the gentle air already redolent with the sweet scent of new-mown hay from the not distant shore. It was as calm and sweet an autumn night as ever falls across the tired earth. The land breeze blew softly across the decks; the bright radiance of the glorious moon of harvest sparkled and wavered and flickered with sinuous, restless brilliancy on the tossing water ahead. All the busy notes of preparation had died away. There had come over the hearts of all, in that moment before the approaching crisis, a little silence which bespoke a recognition of the gravity of the impending conflict. The mellow-toned bell forward was striking the time; two, four, six, seven bells in the second dog watch, half after seven o'clock. The minutes were being rung away for some of the men upon the decks of the great old ship; for many of them the bell would strike no more. Some who had gazed carelessly upon the setting sun would not see it rise again. Laughter ceased, jests failed, and some unwonted lips, while eyes were heavenward turned, murmured the name of God in belated petition. Even the most hardened and indifferent sailor felt the influence of the hour and was still.

Off on the starboard bow, the Pallas was gallantly speeding toward her distant foe. The Alliance, having paid no attention to repeated signals, was still edging in toward the convoy. The Serapis with her topsail to the mast, her men at quarters, ports open, lanterns lighted, was grimly waiting. As Jones's eye fell upon the Alliance, his lips were tightened; a black shadow swept across his face which boded ill for Landais again. When Dale, standing by his side, ventured to break his reverie by a bitter comment upon the defection of the frigate, Jones remarked, —

"Never mind, sir. The fewer we are, the more honor we shall gain by taking them."

But in the main the two officers kept silent watch together. Even the chattering Frenchmen caught the contagion of the portentous moments and stood in quiet ranks prepared and ready. It was no quarrel of theirs, this in which they fought, but their old and ever present hatred of England gave them inspiration enough for the conflict. The breeze freshened

'TWEEN DECKS WITH THE MEN

slightly; and as the Richard drew nearer the Serapis, the latter swung her ponderous main-yard and slowly filled away. The two ships were sailing at right angles to each other, the Richard slightly ahead of the Serapis, which was moving to cross her bow.

"Shall I go to the batteries now, captain?" asked the first lieutenant.

"Yes, I think you would better," answered Jones, stretching out his hand.

"Good-bye, sir," said the other, grasping it firmly.

"Good-bye; God bless you, Richard," said the older man, looking gravely at his beloved subordinate.

"And you, sir," returned Dale, with an unusual accent of tender affection; then he turned and ran rapidly to his station.

"Pass the word quickly," said Jones to young Brooks, "for the men to deliver their fire promptly and together when the word is given. Not a gun is to be discharged until the order. After that, as rapidly as possible."

As the fleet-footed midshipman ran along the decks, a little murmur of excitement arose. There was a shifting of positions; men sprang to their stations; hoarse whispers came from the gun captains, as the smouldering matches, or glowing loggerheads, were handed to them by their subordinates.

"Silence fore and aft the decks!" came the clear voice of the captain.

The murmurs died away as young Brooks sprang up the ladder and reported that everything was ready.

The boy officers choked down something that rose in their throats as they walked nervously up and down their divisions. A fleeting thought they gave to home, mother, hours of play, so far away. It was the first battle for many of them. Down on the berth-deck in front of the hatchway, little Payne looked to the priming of his pistols and whispered a word or two to his men, who stood with their muskets pointing down through the gratings covering the hatchway. He wished he had been up on deck with the rest, fighting a great gun, or attached to the side of the captain; but the captain had told him that the post of honor and importance was here, and here he would stand. There, on the starboard side, his young messmate and friend, McCollin, gave another careful inspection to his three old eighteen-pounders, firmly resolved to give such an account with them, if they did not burst, as would decide the action.

Caswell and Mayrant were in the forecastle to fight the two guns there. Mr. Mease, the purser, as brave a man as ever stepped a deck, though no sailor, had charge of the quarter-deck guns. Stacey, the sailing-master, stood aft by the wheel to assist in working the ship. Brooks and De Chamillard were on the poop near Jones. Fanning, with his bullies in the maintop, was anxiously wishing that he, too, might have a place in the centre of the conflict, the gun-deck, little knowing what decisive moment was in store for him.

They were nearer now, well within gun-shot, yet there was no sound from either ship. The tense

'TWEEN DECKS WITH THE MEN

expectancy of the moment was becoming unbearable to the younger hands. What were the captains of the ships about? Why did n't they fire? Away off on the horizon, flashes of light and the deep boom of artillery reverberating across the water, told that their consort had joined in battle with the Scarborough. Why were they so slow? Suddenly, in the midst of the silence, broken only by the soft sigh of the summer wind through the top-hamper, the splashing of the bluff bows, as they forced themselves through the rippling water, came the sound of a hail from the English ship, the words of which were indistinguishable.

"I don't understand you," cried Jones, then he turned to the quartermaster and said softly, —

"Over with the helm! Hard-a-starboard!" As the wheel was put over by the skilful hands of the quartermaster and his mate, the great ship swung slowly to port and rounded to off the port bow of the English ship.

The Englishman hailed again.

"This is the United States ship Bon Homme Richard," shouted Paul Jones in reply, at the top of his voice, springing up on the rail the while. "Stand by!" A quiver and shiver went through the ship from her tops to her very vitals. "Fire!"

Streams of light leaped out in the darkness; clouds of smoke rose at once from the sides of the Richard only to be met and brushed away by a broadside which had been delivered no less promptly from the English ship. Groans and curses and yells and cheers rose from the blood-stained decks upon which men writhed in the agony of ghastly wounds, or lay contorted in hideous death where they had fallen, for at close range both broadsides had done fearful execution.

The desperate men ran the huge guns in and out and loaded them with frantic energy and kept up a continuous cannonade upon their foes. The roar of the great guns drowned every other sound as the two ships sailed side by side in bitter conflict, but the trained ear of the American captain had detected another sound coincident with the first broadside which told a tale of disaster. When the loggerheads had been applied to the priming of two of the eighteens, they had exploded with a terrific concussion, killing and wounding nearly every man of their crews.

McCollin, who commanded the battery, was struck by a piece of iron and received a dreadful wound. He remained at his post, however, clinging tenaciously to a broken stanchion for a moment until he recovered himself a little. As the frightened and appalled men shrank away from the remaining gun of the battery, not yet discharged in view of the dreadful explosion, he seized the hot iron from the dead hand of the captain of number one gun, and setting his lips grimly staggered over to the last cannon.

"Don't do it, sir!" hoarsely cried the old boatswain's mate who served under him. "It'll blow up with ye, as the others ha' done!" There was no reply. McCollin was beyond words. With set lips

'TWEEN DECKS WITH THE MEN

and grim face, in silence he wavered on before the awe-struck men. With tottering steps he reached the gun and applied the iron. There was a blinding roar and the gun whirled inboard in rapid recoil from the force of the discharge.

"Load it again," said the gasping boy, striving to stop the blood with his hand against his side. Before the men, who, inspired by such heroism, had sprung eagerly forward, could reach the piece, an eighteen-pound shot from the Serapis' lower deck struck it fair and square on the trunnion and dismounted it. That battery was useless. The explosion had made a gaping hole in the side of the Richard, through which the red-lighted side of the Serapis but a short distance away could be seen plainly; the deck above and below was badly shattered by the blowing up of the guns.

"All the men alive of this division," said McCollin, thickly, "will find places at the divisions on the gun-deck. We can do nothing more here. Good-bye, Payne."

A few moments later a powder-blackened, blood-stained, white-faced, desperate little figure appeared out of the smoke before the captain.

"McCollin, you here!" he cried sternly, "why are you not with your battery, sir?"

"I have to report, sir," said the boy, grasping the rail with one hand to keep from falling, while he saluted with the other, "that two of the berth-deck guns blew up, sir, and the other was dismounted. Have you any orders for me, sir?"

"Too bad!" cried Jones. "Orders! — but you are wounded!"

At this moment a round shot struck the lad fair in the chest. With his hand still at salute he was whirled across the deck and thrown against the taffrail, a broken mass of what had been humanity.

"Good Heaven!" exclaimed the captain, staring and almost losing his iron nerve at this double shock, — the loss of the battery and the death of the midshipman. "Poor lad! A hero!"

The ships were nearer now; the rifles of the Frenchmen were cracking and the fire from the great guns was continuous. The Richard had drawn well ahead; and fearful that the Serapis would cross his stern and rake, Jones now shivered his headsails, threw his aftersails aback, checked the way of his own ship, and the Serapis, firing madly into the smoke, drew ahead of the Richard. Jones then put his helm up to try to cross her stern and rake. The quick handling of the English ship frustrated this plan. The bow of the Richard struck the port quarter of the Serapis. The two ships hung together a moment, boarders were called on both sides; but before they could be used, the two ships drifted apart and formed a line ahead, with not a single gun bearing on either ship. The roar of the guns gradually subsided and even the crack of the small arms died away. The smoke drifted slowly off to leeward.

CHAPTER XX

The Indomitable Ego

THE battle had been maintained with the utmost fury for nearly three quarters of an hour, and both ships had sustained severe injuries, the Richard being in much the worse condition. The heavy shot from the long eighteens of the Serapis had played havoc with her. Pearson naturally thought that it was about time for Jones to surrender, though the hour when Jones thought it time to surrender would never strike. The sudden silence which had fallen upon the conflict was broken by a voice from the British ship. In high interrogation it rang over the waters in the moonlight.

"Have you struck?" was the question of the Serapis. From the shattered Richard came Jones's immortal answer, —

"I have not yet begun to fight!"

A roar of wild exultation, a gigantic Homeric laugh, broke from the throats of the crew of the Richard, as the reply of the captain was passed from deck to deck, until the whole ship from truck to keelson quivered with responsive joy. It was a joke, the character of which those blood-stained ruffians could well appreciate; but the captain was in no mood for joking. He was serious, and in the simplicity of the answer lay its greatness. Strike! Not now, nor ever! Beaten! The fighting is but just begun! The preposterous possibility of surrender cannot even be considered. What manner of man this, with whom you battle in the moonlight, brave Pearson? An unfamiliar kind to you, and to most, such as has not been before, nor shall be again. Yet all the world shall see and understand at this time.

"*I have not yet begun to fight!*"

Surprising answer! On a ship shattered beyond repair, her best guns exploded and useless, her crew decimated, ringed about with dead and dying, the captain has not yet begun to fight! But there was no delay after the answer, no philosophizing, no heroics. The man of action was there. He meant business! Every moment when the guns were silent was a wasted one.

The helm was shifted to starboard, and the headsails shivered. The Richard slowly swung off to port and gathered headway again. The Serapis had lost an opportunity of tacking and raking. In order more quickly to bring his guns to bear and perhaps to prevent a raking by the enemy, Captain Pearson threw all aback; and the two ships, one backing, and the other reaching ahead, slowly drew abreast each other, the batteries speaking again as soon as the guns bore. The wind was very light, and the motion of both ships was sluggish in the extreme, so that they practically lay side by side, steerage way almost gone, slowly drifting in for long minutes, until there came a sudden, temporary breath of wind.

THE INDOMITABLE EGO

The position was most advantageous for the Serapis, as with her heavier and more numerous guns she could deliberately knock the Richard into a "cocked hat." She was much the speedier and handier ship, and might reasonably hope to choose her own distance, and, having selected a point of vantage, maintain it to the end. Pearson's game was to fight at long range until he had sunk his enemy; no difficult task that last, — she was half sinking now! But what the Richard lacked in mobility and direction, she made up in her captain. Jones did things instinctively; Pearson had to think about them. Jones's only hope was in getting to close quarters and making use of the disciplined French soldiery upon his decks.

They had done good service already in clearing the spar-deck of the English. Therefore, as the Richard, gathering way, gradually forged ahead, her helm was shifted to port and the vessel slowly swung across the bow of the Serapis, which had just begun to fill away again, as Pearson saw that he had nearly backed out of action. The bow of the Serapis struck the starboard quarter of the Richard, the jibboom thrusting itself violently through the mizzen rigging. There was a terrific crash at the moment of impact; and a second later the English, cheering frantically, jumped upon the heel of the bowsprit and clambered upon the rail of their ship.

They were led by a tall distinguished-looking officer, who attracted double attention, as he wore the red uniform of the English army. As their heads appeared over the rail, the powerful voice of Jones could be heard shouting, "Boarders away!" Not waiting for the men who came springing up on the quarter-deck in obedience to his summons, the dauntless captain seized a pike from the rack and hurled it through the air at the leader of the Englishmen. Good fortune guided his hand, and the steel head of the lance struck fair in the bosom of the soldier. The British wavered a moment as their officer fell, and Jones discharged his pistols full among them. Then De Chamillard and those of his marines left alive upon the deck, by a well-directed point-blank volley, drove back the boarding party of the English.

The two ships were grinding against each other, and the wind on the aftersail of the Serapis slowly forced her around until she swung parallel to the Richard. The jibboom snapped off short under the strain, and her starboard anchor caught in the tangled rigging of the American frigate; and Stacey, the sailing-master, sprang to lash the ships together. Stacey snatched a rope from the raffle on the deck and strove to overhaul it. It was tangled, and he found great difficulty in clearing it. An impatient man at best, and now greatly excited, he swore roundly as he tugged at the vexatious rope.

"Don't swear, Mr. Stacey," said Jones, calmly, coming to his assistance "In another moment we may all be in eternity, but let us do our duty."

With his own hands Jones passed the lashing.

On the gun-deck below, the batteries were being fought fiercely. The two ships were lying side by

THE INDOMITABLE EGO

side, one heading in, the other out, the bow of one by the stern of the other, the starboard side of the Serapis closely touching the starboard side of the Richard. In the hope that the Richard would drift clear, Captain Pearson now dropped his port anchor; in vain, no bull-dogs ever clung to foes with more tenacity of grip than did those two ships in deadly grapple joined together. The Richard and the Serapis were fast locked for good, and the two ships swung to the tidal current, the wind being again almost entirely killed. In that position they lay for the next two hours, or until the battle was over.

As the Englishman had not hitherto engaged on the starboard side, the port shutters had not been opened, and the close contact of the two ships rendered it impossible to open them then. The Serapis' men were therefore compelled to fire through them, blowing off the port-lids. It was necessary for the men on both ships to extend the long handles of the rammers and sponges of the guns through the ports into the other ship in order to properly load their own cannon. Badinage of a character easily to be imagined passed back and forth between the two crews, though nothing interrupted the steady and persistent discharge of the batteries. The battle below was literally a hand-to-hand conflict with great guns, all the advantages in number and size being with the English.

At this juncture a new note was added to the conflict. Jones, whose eyes were everywhere in the battle, observed a black shadow come darting athwart the two fighting ships, shutting off the moonlight. It was the Alliance.

"Ah!" he said to himself, "Landais has seen the folly of his disobedience and has come to our assistance."

As the American ship, with her French captain and half-English crew, loomed up between him and the bright moon, he thought of course that she would range down upon the unengaged side of the Serapis, and with a few broadsides compel her to strike at once. But no, the Alliance under full sail stood on. Her men were at quarters, ports triced up, lanterns lighted. She was passing the bow of the Serapis now. Why did she not fire? The insane and treacherous Landais held steadily on until he was standing squarely across the stern of the Richard. Now she was drawing past them as well. A command rang out. Good God! What was that?

Jones was well-nigh petrified with astonishment when at short range the Alliance poured in a raking broadside, of which the Richard received the brunt, though it was apparently discharged impartially at the two ships. As Landais drew past the stern, the helm of the Alliance was shifted. She swung parallel to the Richard, poured in another broadside, circled the Richard forward, and raked her again! The last discharge was a frightful one. The shot at close range swept the crowded decks of the American ship, which seemed actually to quiver and flinch at this treacherous blow. This broadside did much damage, killing and wounding many on the forecastle, among

THE INDOMITABLE EGO

them Midshipman Caswell, mortally. Shrieks, groans, and cries of startled surprise and dismay rose with increasing volume from the ship.

"The Alliance, the Alliance — "

"We are betrayed! We are betrayed!"

"The English have got the ship!" came from every side in wild confusion.

"This is the Richard," shouted Jones at the top of his voice at the first fire. "Hold your fire! Show the private signals there!" he cried hastily to the faithful Brooks; but the Alliance paid no attention to these and other warning cries. As the three broadsides were delivered by the American frigate, the men, in their perfectly excusable terror at this treacherous blow in the back, actually began to break from their quarters and leave the guns. That was never to be thought of under any circumstances.

"Back!" shouted Jones, promptly. "Back to your quarters, every mother's son of you! Shoot the first man that flinches from the guns!" Dale and De Weibert and the midshipman gallantly seconded his orders; and the Alliance, sailing away toward the Pallas and delivering no more shot upon them, the conflict was resumed. That the men could be got to the guns again after this frightfully unsettling attack, was a supreme testimony to the quality of their officers, and to their own as well.

Indeed, upon the part of the Serapis the battle had never been intermitted. The long eighteens of her main battery had simply silenced and dismounted, knocked to pieces, and put out of action nearly all the twelves on the main-deck of the Richard. The starboard side of the American had been beaten in, and the port side beaten out by the heavy fire at close range until the British were literally firing through a hole; the shot hurtling through the air and falling harmlessly in the water far on the farther side. The underpinning of the upper decks of the ship was of course nearly knocked to pieces. Why the decks did not fall in and the whole thing collapse was a mystery.

There had been no fighting at all on the berth-deck since the bursting of the three guns, but poor little Payne had hung grimly to his post. One by one the men of the guarding squad had been picked off by stray shot until there were none left but he and the master-at-arms. Several shot from the British had entered below the water-line of the Richard, and she was making water fast. There was nearly four feet of water in the hold then, and it was rising. The prisoners below were in a wild state of terror. Imprecations, curses, appeals, had come up through the gratings over the hatchway, to which the young man had turned a deaf year.

To the other dangers of the battle, fire now added its devastating touch. In fact, both ships were aflame in several places. The burning gun-wads had lodged in the chains and other inflammable positions, and writhing, tossing, serpent-like torches threw their hot light over the scene of terror. As the smoke drifted down the hatchway, the prisoners in the hold could stand it no longer. There was a sudden rush below

THE INDOMITABLE EGO

toward the opening; the gratings were splintered and broken by the thrust of a piece of timber; a head or two appeared in the clear; hands clutched at the combings.

"Back!" shouted Payne, trying to steady his boyish voice.

"No! D—n your baby face!" shouted the first prisoner, furiously, clutching desperately at the combing, while he was being lifted up in the arms of the men below. "D'ye think we'll stay here and be drowned like bloody rats in a hole!"

With white lips and a sinking heart the boy thrust his pistol full into the man's face, and with a trembling finger pulled the trigger. He did the like to the next man with a second pistol. To seize the musket of a dead marine and point it at the third, was the work of a second. Awed by this resolution and the promptitude of his action, the other prisoners fell back for the time. The sweat stood out on the forehead of the young midshipman. He had shot a man — two men — in cold blood! It seemed like murder. But he had done his duty. The words of the captain rang in his ear: "*Keep them down!*"

It was hot — hot as hell — on the berth-deck. The smoke poured in thick, suffocating clouds between decks. The wavering reflections from the flames on every side accentuated the horror. Bands of men flitted by ghost-like, here and there, with buckets of water, striving to fight the flames; lances of light leaped across the deck from the protruding muzzles of the guns on the Serapis, piercing the

THE GRIP OF HONOR

gloomy darkness with angry flashes. Bullets, grape, splinters of timber, solid shot, bits of torn humanity, whistled past his head. He was wild, crazy; the hugeness of the tragedy about him oppressed him direfully. There was a weight in his bosom, a choking in his throat; the bitter, acrid taste of the burned powder was in his mouth; the sickening smell of reeking blood pervaded his being; he longed to throw down his weapon and fly, anywhere, to get a respite from the infernal demand upon him. But he was a sailor, the son of a race of fighters. He held on. The deep roar of the guns above him told him that the battle was still going on. Suddenly out of the smoke appeared the burly form of the carpenter, wounded, blotched with red and gray, leaping forward, crying in terror-stricken accents, —

"We're sinking! we're sinking! Four feet of water in the hold!"

The gunner and his mates, apparently equally terrified, came running from the magazines as they caught the contagion of the moment. They sprang to the gun-deck and thence to the spar-deck, repeating the carpenter's cry, "We're sinking! we're sinking! Quarter! Quarter!"

"We must release the prisoners!" cried the master-at-arms, turning toward the little officer.

"Not while I live!" said Payne, resolutely, all his courage coming back to him in a moment.

"The ship is sinking; the battle is lost; make way!" returned the burly master-at-arms, springing toward the hatchway.

THE INDOMITABLE EGO

"Back!" cried the midshipman, fiercely, pointing his musket at him; the boy's blood was up now. "Here they stay, and here we stay! The orders of the captain —"

He never finished his words; a grape-shot struck him fair in the forehead. The master-at-arms tore open the hatch-cover.

"On deck!" he cried; "the ship is sinking!"

In panic terror, crowding and trampling upon each other like a mob of wild beasts, the maddened prisoners scrambled up the hatchway, and, yelling like animals, ran pell-mell for the gun-deck. The body of the brave midshipman was spurned, crushed, and broken beneath their feet as they ran.

CHAPTER XXI

The Audacity of Despair

ON the spar-deck things had gone better. Though De Chamillard and his marines had been driven from the poop by the fire of the English, the men in the tops had more than evened that reverse. As the two ships lay side by side, the interlocking yards made a convenient bridge from one to the other, over which a bold man might pass. It happened that some of the choicest spirits on the Richard were stationed in the maintop. Fanning, who had been busily engaged with small arms, saw his opportunity. As the little parties in the two tops exchanged volleys, the midshipman threw his men on the yard; and as the smoke cleared away, the astonished British saw the Americans rushing toward them.

The first and second men were shot down and fell to the deck of the Serapis; the third, a gigantic man, by a desperate leap gained a foothold in the top. Before he was cut down, Fanning and another had joined him over the futtock shrouds; two men took the defenders in the rear by way of the lubber's hole; the rest came swarming. The force of their rush carried everything before it. The English, unable to stand the irresistible onset, were

THE AUDACITY OF DESPAIR

shot down or thrown out of the top. No quarter was asked or given. The Americans, having effected this lodgement in the maintop of the Serapis, now turned their fire upon the fore and mizzen tops, and enabled boarding parties from their own ship to gain possession of all the upper works of the enemy.

It was at this moment that the gunner and the carpenter reached the deck, crying that the ship was sinking and proffering surrender. The gunner ran aft shrieking, "Quarter! Quarter!" intending to lower the flag. Jones, who had been superintending the working of the quarter-deck guns, which were without an officer since Mease, who had been fighting heroically, had been severely wounded, of course heard the noise, and turning about saw the gunner running for the flag. Fortunately the flag had been shot away; and as the gunner was seeking it, fumbling over the halliards in the darkness, Pearson, hearing the cries, called out again, —

"Do you ask for quarter?"

Jones had taken two long leaps across the deck to the side of the gunner. Seizing his discharged pistol, he brought the butt of it heavily down upon the forehead of the man, cracking his skull and silencing him forever.

"Never!" he shouted in reply to the Englishman.

"Then I will give none!" said Pearson, — an entirely superfluous remark, by the way.

It was at this juncture that the "Alliance" was seen coming down again as before. Jones had time but for one glance of apprehension when he heard the noise of the leaping prisoners below. He sprang to the main hatch.

"The prisoners have been released," cried De Weibert, meeting him; the Frenchman had been toiling like a hero on the gun-deck. "The battery is silenced, we have not a single gun to work, the ship is afire! We must yield!" he exclaimed.

As the frightened men came crowding up the hatchways, Dale, who had just fired the only remaining gun on the deck that was left fit for action, took in the situation at once. He stayed the rush in the nick of time by voice and action. He sprang into the midst of them, threatening them, striking them, beating them down, driving them back with his sword. It was a magnificent display of hardihood and courage, presence of mind and resource.

"To the pumps!" he cried with prompt decision. "For your lives, men! The English ship is sinking, and we'll go down with her unless you can keep us afloat!" he shouted in thunder tones with superb audacity. The battle lost was won again in that minute.

"Well done, Richard!" shouted Jones, leaping through the hatchway and seconding the daring ruse of his noble lieutenant by his own mighty voice and herculean efforts, crying masterfully, "Get to the pumps, men! Lively! for God's sake! The ship is sinking under your feet! The English ship is going!"

It was unparalleled assurance, but it won. The

THE AUDACITY OF DESPAIR

two officers actually succeeded in forcing the English prisoners to man the pumps, where they worked with a frantic energy born of their persistent daze of terror. This left the regular crew of the ship free to fight the fires and to do what they could with the remaining guns. As Jones sprang back to the quarter-deck, the surgeon, covered with blood, and appalled at the carnage, came running toward him, crying, —

"The ship is sinking, sir! The cock-pit is under water! I have no place to stow the wounded. We must surrender!"

"Strike! Strike!" cried De Chamillard, who was wounded. "We can do no more!"

"What, gentlemen!" cried Jones, "would you have me strike to a drop of water and a bit of fire? Up, De Chamillard! Here, doctor, help me get this gun over."

The surgeon hesitated, looked around again, and, not liking the appearance of things about him, turned and ran below. Not to his station, for that was under water. His mates had been killed. He wandered up and down the decks, doing what he could — which was but little — for the wounded where they lay. Assisted by two or three of the seamen, with his own hands Jones dragged one of the nine-pounders from the disengaged side of the deck across to the starboard side to take the place of a dismounted one; and, while the heavy battery of the Serapis continued its unavailing fire below, these three small guns under his personal direction concentrated their fire upon the mainmast of the Serapis.

The fortuitous position of the Americans in the enemy's tops enabled them to pour a perfect rain of small-arm fire upon the spar-deck of the Serapis with little possibility of effective return. Man after man was shot down by the side of the intrepid Pearson, who, whatever his other lack of qualifications, showed that he possessed magnificent personal courage, until he remained practically alone upon the deck, — alone, and as yet undaunted.

It is impossible to describe the scene. It is not within the power of words to portray the situation, after over two hours of the most frightful and determined combat. No two ships were ever in such condition; no battle that was ever fought was like it. The decks were covered with dead and dying; bands of men in different directions were fighting the fires; the smoke in lowering clouds hung heavily over the ships, for the wind had died and there was scarcely enough to blow it away. The pale moonlight mingled with the red glare from the flames and threw an added touch of lurid ghastliness trembling over the smoke-wrapt sea. From below came the steady roar of the Serapis' guns, from above the continuous crackling of the Richard's small arms. The noises blended in a hideous diapason of destruction, which rose to an offended Heaven in the horrid discord of an infernal region. The prisoners, still under the influence of their terror, toiled at the clanking pumps. The water gushed redly from the

THE AUDACITY OF DESPAIR

bleeding scuppers. Order, tactics, discipline, had been forgotten. Men glared with blood-shot eyes, set their teeth beneath foam-flaked lips, and fought where they stood, — fought in frenzy against whatever came to hand, whether it was the English ship, or the roaring flames, or the rushing waters. They recked nothing of consequences. In their frantic battle-lust they beat upon the sides of the other ship with their bare hands and bloody knuckles, and knew not what they did. Their breath came quick and short; the red of battle was before their vision; they had but one thought. Slay! Kill! One would have said that the brute instinct was uppermost in every heart. But in scenes of this kind it is not the greatest brute that wins, but the greatest soul; and the one man who still preserved his calmness in this orgy of war was the man to win the battle — Jones.

The Alliance had repeated her previous performance, but the men had been worked to such a pitch that they never heeded her; many of them did not know of it. Both ships were thoroughly beaten. It was only a question as to which would realize it first, who would first surrender. Nay, there was no question whatever of Jones' surrender under any circumstances whatsoever. Pearson would give up under some conditions, and those had at last arrived. That was the essential difference between the two men; it was radical.

CHAPTER XXII

Sinking, but Triumphant

AND now happened the incident which finally decided the battle. By Jones's orders, quantities of hand grenades, a small, highly combustible, and explosive shell, about the size of a large apple, had been placed in the tops. After the battle in mid-air by which the Americans had gained possession, he shouted out that they be used in accordance with his instructions. Fanning sent a man with a bucket of grenades out on the extreme end of the main-yard-arm. Wrapping his legs around the yard, he sat down, and leaning against the lift, deliberately threw his bomb-shells, one by one, down the open main hatchway of the Serapis. The powder boys of the latter ship had been bringing charges of powder for the various guns from the magazine; and as many of the guns had been put out of action by the American fire, the supply had been greater than the demand. A large pile had been carelessly allowed to accumulate upon the deck. One of the grenades carromed against the hatch combing, and fell into the centre of the charges.

There was a detonating crash, so loud, so terrific, that it actually seemed to blow even the roar of the battle into eternity. Twenty or thirty men were

SINKING, BUT TRIUMPHANT

killed or badly wounded, many of them torn to atoms, by the explosion, and the rest of the men on the Englishman's deck were dazed and driven from their stations by the concussion. The clothes of many were actually ripped from their bodies, so that they stood naked and wondering, though they were otherwise unhurt. A long moment of ghastly silence succeeded this accident on the Serapis. Men everywhere paused with bated breath to wait the issue. The Serapis, dragging the Richard, reeled and rocked under the shock. It was a last catastrophe which broke the strength of Pearson's endurance and ended his resistance. He could fight no more. Was it the devil himself who commanded the other ship? The English captain sprang aft to the mizzenmast. A great English standard had been nailed to the timber of the spar. With his own hands he tore it down. The battle was over! At the same moment the mainmast of the Serapis undermined, and, eaten away in its heart by the gnawing attack of the quarter-deck guns of the Richard, came crashing down, a hopeless ruin, carrying some of the Americans into eternity as it fell.

"*They have struck their flag!*" cried Jones, who had sprung upon the rail at the moment of the explosion and had witnessed Pearson's action. "Cease firing!"

His voice rang through the ship with such a note of proud triumph as has rarely been heard within the fought over confines of the narrow seas.

"They have struck; the ship is ours!" ran from

man to man among the Americans. Wild cheers broke into the night in an ever-increasing volume of sound.

"Send Mr. Dale to me," said Jones to young Brooks as the flag came down. The midshipman had been wounded, but still kept his station.

As Dale came running toward his captain, Jones cried, —

"Muster a boarding party and take charge of the prize; the fight is over!"

But no, the battle was not over. A few moments before, an English ship captain among the prisoners had succeeded in escaping through the rents in the shattered sides of the two ships and had told the plight of the Richard to the first lieutenant of the Serapis. With this information the men on the gun-deck had been rallied, and led by their officers had returned to their quarters and had resumed the battle. They, too, were heroes. Mayrant, who ran aft from the forecastle as he saw Pearson strike his flag, jumped on the rail by Jones's orders and followed Dale upon the deck of the English ship. Such was the confusion of the moment that as Mayrant leaped on the deck he was actually run through the thigh by a pike in the hand of a wounded British sailor. Pearson was standing alone as if dazed, on the quarter-deck of his ship, holding one clenched hand against his breast, with the other grasping his trailing flag. In his face was that look of defeat and despair which is the saddest aspect of baffled impotent humanity.

SINKING, BUT TRIUMPHANT

"Have you struck, sir?" cried Dale, stopping before the English captain.

"Yes," was the grim reply; his voice was a broken whisper indicating in the tones his mental agony.

"I am come to take possession."

"Very good, sir," said Pearson, bitterly, as before, and dropping the flag; then he reached for his sword.

Just at this moment, Pascoe, the first lieutenant of the Serapis, came bounding up the hatchway from the deck below.

"A few more broadsides, sir, and they are ours," he cried impetuously. "They are in a sinking—"

"The ship has struck, sir, and you are my prisoner," interrupted Dale, quickly, seeing the necessity of promptitude.

"Struck! This ship! Your prisoner!" cried the astonished Englishman.

"Yes, sir. Your sword!" demanded Dale. The man hesitated.

"Disarm him!" cried the American. Two or three of the boarding parties closed around them.

"Sir," asked the lieutenant, turning to his captain, "is it true that we have struck?"

"Yes, sir," answered Pearson, hoarsely.

"My God!" cried Pascoe. There was a momentary silence.

"I have nothing more to say, sir," he added. "I will go below and call off the men," said the lieutenant, turning away.

"No, sir!" interrupted Dale. "You will accompany your captain on board our ship at once. Pass the word to cease firing. The ship has struck."

As the English captain and his first lieutenant stepped over the rail upon the high poop of the Richard, the roar of the guns died away, this time for good. Seizing a dangling rope they swung themselves inboard, and found themselves face to face with a little man in a tattered uniform, hatless, covered with dust and smoke, powder-stained and grimy with the soil of the battle. Blood spattering from a wound in his forehead had coagulated upon his cheek. He was a hideous-looking spectacle. The red firelight played luridly upon him. Nothing but the piercing black eyes which burned and gleamed out of his face in the darkness bespoke the high humanity of the man.

"Is it —"

"Captain John Paul Jones, at your service, gentlemen."

"My sword," said Pearson, tendering it to him formally. "I regret," he added ungraciously, "at being compelled to strike to a man who has fought with a halter around his neck."

"Sir," said Jones, with a magnanimity as great as his valor, "you have fought like a hero, and I make no doubt that your sovereign will reward you in the most ample manner. Mr. Brooks, escort these gentlemen to my cabin."

And which was the gentleman then?

The two ships were now cut adrift, Dale remaining on the Serapis to take command. He had sat down

SINKING, BUT TRIUMPHANT

a moment for rest, and as he attempted to rise to his feet he fell to the deck, discovering only in that way that he had been severely wounded,—a thing which had escaped his notice in the heat of the action.

By the most heroic efforts of the prize crew on the Serapis and the remaining men on the Richard, the English prisoners were driven back into the hold, the flames subdued, and some semblance of order restored. Cottineau had captured the Pallas after an hour of good hard fighting, and the victory was entirely with the Americans. But it had been purchased at a fearful cost. There is no battle on land or sea in the world's history where the percentage of loss was greater than the battle between the Serapis and the Richard.

About seventy per cent on the Serapis and over fifty per cent on the Richard had been killed or wounded, and the Bon Homme Richard was in a sinking condition. She had been literally beaten to pieces. It was not safe to remain upon her decks. Consequently the prisoners and the wounded, groaning and crying in anguish, were removed to the Serapis. In the early morning of the day following, the brave ship which had earned undying immortality in her worn-out old age, because for three brief hours John Paul Jones and his men had battled upon her decks, sank forever beneath the sea. The great battle-flag under which she had fought had been reset, and fluttered above her as she went down.

The refitting of the prizes for the returning voyage

was at once begun. To anticipate events, it is recorded that Captain Landais, the jealous and false-hearted Frenchman who had so treacherously manœuvred the Alliance, was subsequently court-martialled and dismissed from the service. He should have been hanged from her highest yard-arm.

BOOK VI
THE HAND OF GOD

CHAPTER XXIII

On Board the Serapis again

"THE battle is on," said O'Neill, in the small boat, to Elizabeth, "and I am not there. Oh, God, give us a little breeze!" he cried. In anticipation he swung the oars inboard, stepped the mast once more, letting the sail hang, and then resumed his place by her side.

"God is good to me," she said at last. "He will not let you be there to be killed. You have had trouble enough, and have run enough risks. He wishes to keep you for me." He shook his head.

"My place is there; my duty is on yonder deck. Would that I had returned to the ship without going up to the castle!"

"Why, then," she said reproachfully, "you would not have seen me!"

"I know," he replied, "but then I would be in my rightful place, fighting where I should be; Coventry would be honored in doing his duty; the admiral would be happy; your marriage would take place—"

"And you," she cried, womanlike, placing him in the balance, as opposed to all the rest,—"would you have been happy?"

"Happiness has nothing to do with that," he an-

THE GRIP OF HONOR

swered impatiently; "it is a question of duty. I have been a fool."

"Has the fool been rewarded in accordance with his folly?" she asked him. "Nay, look at me before you reply," she cried imperiously, turning his head until his eyes looked into her own. In the face of that girl, in the limpid light of her magic glance, in that mystic night, there was but one answer to be made.

"I say no more," he replied, kissing her softly. "You are right. I have you. You are worth it all. I will try to be a philosopher about all the rest."

Meanwhile the intermittent reports had been succeeded by a steady roar of artillery which reverberated and rolled along the surface of the water. The Scarborough, some distance from the Serapis and the Richard to the northwest, was apparently hotly engaged with the Pallas; while the Alliance seemed to be sailing back and forth between the two groups of combatants, pouring in a random fire upon friend and foe alike. Great clouds of smoke, punctured by vivid flashes of light, overhung the ships.

Back on the heights above the town the people swarmed. O'Neill could picture the old admiral walking up and down the terrace, glass in hand, while he surveyed the battle. There seemed to be little manœuvring going on between the ships, except on the part of the Alliance, and the combat seemed to be a yard-arm to yard-arm fight. Once or twice the roar of the battle died away temporarily, and the smoke blowing off to leeward disclosed the

ON BOARD THE SERAPIS AGAIN

two ships side by side. Sometimes great wreaths of flame, which told that one or the other ship had been set on fire, would leap up into the air.

The feelings of the young officer can be imagined. Adrift in that little boat, watching the awful combat, not even the presence of the woman he loved could compensate him for his absence, in spite of his attempted philosophy. The fever of the conflict possessed him. His breath came hard; the sweat stood on his forehead. He prayed as never before for a breeze to take him to the fight. He murmured incoherent words which told to the tender listener something of the terrible struggle which raged within his bosom. So the long hours wore away.

Toward eleven o'clock they heard a terrific explosion, and then the roar of the battle slackened, and finally died away. When the smoke drifted off, the two ships were lying side by side. Further off, almost hull down, were the Scarborough and the Pallas, who had ceased their fight some time before. The battle was over. Who had won? It was a question he could not answer.

But it was late, and the breeze so long wished for now sprung up once more, and the little boat gathered way and began to slip through the water again. The sky had become overcast; it grew very dark; the wind freshened steadily, and finally blew so strong that it required all the skill and address of which O'Neill was possessed to keep his unsteady little craft from capsizing. Finally he was forced to drop the sail and take to the oars to keep afloat at all. About two o'clock in the morning a squall of rain came down, and they lost sight of the ships. Toward morning the wind moderated again, and they were enabled to set sail once more. But the ocean was covered with a dense mist; they were in the thick of it, and could see nothing. As nearly as he could judge without the aid of a compass, O'Neill headed the boat toward the place where they had last made out the two ships.

"We ought to pick them up in a few moments now," he said to the cowering, frightened, exhausted girl crouching down in the stern sheets in her wet, sodden garments, which clung to her shivering figure. The night had been too much for her; her physical strength had almost given way, though nothing could abate the affection he saw shining still in her tired eyes. "Therefore, in a few moments we shall know our fate."

"How is that?" she said, rousing herself a little.

"If Commodore Jones has been captured," he answered, "I have but to give myself up and redeem Coventry and — you know the rest."

"Yes," she replied wearily and listlessly; "let it come. We have fought a good fight, you and I; we can do no more; and the other alternative?"

"Why, in that case," he said, "we shall be there, under our own flag; he, too, will be saved, and the rest of our troubles are over."

"What think you of the prospect?" she asked, brightening a little.

"It is difficult to say. The Serapis and the Scar-

ON BOARD THE SERAPIS AGAIN

borough should easily be more than a match for our whole squadron. The Richard is almost worthless as a fighting ship, as I said. Landais, who commands the Alliance, is insane. I can't prophesy what Cottineau will do with the Pallas. We have but one advantage."

"And is that a great one?"

"The greatest; it may have decided the battle in our favor."

"What is that, then?" she asked.

"It is not 'what,' but 'who,'" he answered, smiling.

"Who, then?"

"John Paul Jones himself! He alone is worth a thousand."

The light from the rising sun, assisted by the fitful wind, began to dispel the mists of the morning.

"See!" cried the girl, pointing. "There, right ahead of us! Are not those the sails of a ship? What ship?"

Wraithlike, as she pointed at a rift in the mist, and wreathed in clouds of vapor, there appeared, for a second, the light canvas of a great ship. Following her outstretched finger, he caught a fleeting glimpse of it, but saw nothing to reassure him as to the result of the battle; the sight struck terror to his heart. Such canvas as that was never set above the decks of the Richard. As he looked the mist closed around them again; the ship had vanished.

"Ah, 't is gone, but I am certain I saw it. Which

was it?" she continued, hastily rousing herself at the prospect of decision. "'T is a ship, is it not? But which one?"

"The mist is thinning again. 'T will clear away in a moment," he answered evasively. "We shall see more distinctly then; she was making toward us, I think." He could not bear to dash her hopes with the assurance that it was not the Richard, though he had resigned himself to death in consequence of his glimpse at once. It was useless to try to fly; the mist was rising in every direction, and before they could have gone a hundred yards they would be visible to the ship in front of them, now shoving her huge bulk through the thinning clouds of vapor which enshrouded her. The next moment it rolled away. The sunlight flooded the heavens in transformation; the breeze tossed the sea into a thousand white-capped waves. It was morning. Some one on the ship saw the little boat with its two occupants at once; an officer leaped to the rail.

"Boat ahoy!" rang out over the water. The great white frigate, deep sunken, as if deeply laden, was moving sluggishly through the water, and was almost upon them.

"The ship!" screamed the girl, wildly.

"It is the Serapis!" answered O'Neill, in a hollow voice.

"Ah!" she said, sinking back exhausted. "After all, it is over. I shall never survive you."

"Boat ahoy, there!" again cried the officer, standing on the rail, pistol in hand. "Answer my hail, or I fire. Who are you?"

"I am your prisoner, escaped last night from that ship," cried O'Neill. "I wish to deliver myself up."

"Come alongside, then," said the officer, turning inboard and giving a sharp command. The way of the ship was checked; she was thrown up into the wind, and as her broadside slowly swung opposite O'Neill, he saw that her mainmast was gone and that she was frightfully cut up, and bore evidence of having participated in a tremendous action. Away off to the northeast a little cluster of ships were seen on the horizon, too far off to distinguish them. There was no sign of the Richard that he could see. In a few seconds the boat was brought alongside the gangway. Elizabeth clambered up the ladder with his assistance, and they stepped upon the decks. A frightful scene presented itself.

Upon one side amidships, dead men, half-naked, covered with coagulated blood, were literally piled up in a great heap. The deck itself was covered with grime and blood; and a handful of men, most of them wounded in some way, were distributed about the ship, endeavoring to effect some restoration to order. Guns here and there were dismounted; ropes cut in every direction were lying entangled in wild confusion about the fife-rails and masts. The broken mainmast thrust its jagged end a few feet into the air, above the deck; the rest of it was gone.

Spars everywhere were shattered, and great rifts

appeared in the flapping canvas. The rail and bulwarks were broken and smashed on every side. There was not a single boat left swinging at the davits. Splintered woodwork showed where numberless shots had taken effect, and charred pieces of timber on every hand added heartbreaking evidence of conflagration's devastating touch. From the depths beneath the deck came low groans and murmurs of pain, accentuated by the sharp shriek of some deeper sufferer, or the delirious raving of some fevered patient. Elizabeth shrank back appalled.

"How horrible!" she murmured. "Take me away; I cannot stand it!" He caught her in his arms; a little more, and she would have fainted.

"Good heavens!" he said. "In all my battles I never saw such a ship! What a frightful scene! They didn't get off without a fight," he added slowly. An officer, with head bound up in a handkerchief and his arm in a sling, was approaching them.

"Sir," said O'Neill, saluting the while, "I am the officer who escaped last night. I deliver myself up to — Why, it's Stacey!" he cried, in great surprise, recognizing a brother officer of the Richard. "What do you here, man?"

"'Fore Gad, it's O'Neill!" cried the other. "Glad are we to see you, man. But this lady — this is no place for her."

"She goes with me," said O'Neill, briefly. "But you?"

"This is where I belong."

"And they have captured you, I suppose?"

ON BOARD THE SERAPIS AGAIN

"No; the ship is ours."

"And the old Richard?" cried O'Neill.

"Abandoned and sunk after the surrender," answered the young officer. "She was cut to pieces by the Serapis's fire, but we have this ship."

"Thank God!" answered O'Neill, fervently. "And Captain Jones?"

"Aft there on the quarter-deck."

"Come, Elizabeth," he cried, seizing her by the arm; and, he assisting her, they made their way with difficulty, in the confusion, to the quarter-deck.

"Ah, O'Neill, thank God I see you alive again!" said Jones, springing forward, his face beaming. "We got there in time, then, I see."

"Yes, sir, thanks to this lady," answered O'Neill, pointing to Elizabeth.

"Madam, you are fit for a sailor's bride," said the little captain.

"'T is high praise, sir, from Captain Jones, I protest," she answered, rallying herself in the relief of assured safety.

"Would God that I had been with you in this battle!" cried O'Neill, gloomily.

"We missed you. I wished often for you," answered the captain. "The poor old Richard was torn to pieces under our feet. We could not stay on her longer, so we had to come here."

"And I not there! I suppose that I have forfeited everything forever for going up to the castle. Shall you break me, sir?"

THE GRIP OF HONOR

"Nothing, nothing, shall be done, my poor boy," answered the captain, kindly. "You have been punished enough by not having been with us in the greatest battle ever fought on the sea. But it seems to me you have not entirely lost the game. You, too, have a prize in tow. How go your love affairs?" he whispered.

"Well, indeed, sir; the Lady Elizabeth is here, as you see. We are to be married at once, sir."

"You may have the chaplain of the Serapis for that purpose."

"Yes, sir. When he last officiated for me, he was reading my funeral service," replied O'Neill, smiling.

"Some people would say it's much the same thing," laughed the captain; "but we know better. Ah well, that's over now, thank God; and this lady — Madam," he said, turning to her, "I bade you welcome to a ship once before. It is a different ship now, but the welcome is just the same."

"Know you aught of Major Edward Coventry, Captain Jones?" cried Elizabeth. This time it was she who remembered.

"Why, he lies on the deck yonder, dying. He wouldn't let me take him below. Do you know — but I forgot, he was your friend."

"Take me to him!" she cried hastily, and in a moment she was kneeling by his side. They had made him as comfortable as possible with cushions and boat cloaks, but his hours were numbered. His head was thrown back, his face ghastly pale. Blood-

ON BOARD THE SERAPIS AGAIN

stained the linen of his shirt about his breast. His eyes were closed; the end was at hand.

"Poor fellow!" said O'Neill, in great sorrow, "he died for me;" and then he briefly recounted the circumstances of their escape to the astonished captain.

"Do you know how he was wounded, sir?" he asked.

"It was my own hand that struck the blow," answered Jones. "Would it had been otherwise! There was a moment in the action when they sprang to board. He leaped upon the rail, cutlass in hand; he was a fair and easy mark; I met them with a pike, which I buried in his bosom. He fell back smiling. I remember that I thought it strange to see him smiling at that time, even in the heat of the battle — too bad — too bad!" he said.

"Oh, Edward!" cried the girl, tears streaming down her face, "I never thought to see you thus! I never meant to bring you to this! If you could but speak to me — to say that you forgave me for it all! If I could have your blessing before — " The man stirred a little and opened his eyes. He looked about him vacantly, but consciousness began to dawn again, and with the dawn came recognition. It was the face of Elizabeth bending over him. She was the woman whom he loved. There, back of her, was O'Neill. He began to comprehend.

"Elizabeth," he murmured, "my death — not in vain — then."

"Forgive me — forgive me," she cried brokenly. "Oh, forgive me! I did love you!"

"Yes," he said, faintly smiling; "but — not like — "

He glanced at O'Neill. "You, too!" he murmured; "make — her — happy." His mind wandered a little. "Father," he cried suddenly, "don't look at me in that way! I did it because I loved her; her happiness before mine."

"Oh, doctor, can nothing be done; is there no hope?" cried O'Neill to the attending surgeon.

"Nothing, sir. 'T will not be long now," answered the surgeon, shaking his head.

CHAPTER XXIV

Not Guilty, my Lord

"THERE'S a boat comin' alongside, sir," said a midshipman to Captain Jones, "flying an admiral's flag."

"Ah, that will be our friend Lord Westbrooke," he said, turning toward the gangway. "Show him to me if he comes on board." Elizabeth knelt by the side of the dying man, who had sunk into silence again, and bathed his head with her handkerchief, while the doctor applied some simple restorative. In a moment the stately form of the old admiral stepped through the gangway, and he looked about him in astonishment.

"God bless me, what a fight! I knew that rebel was a desperate man, but I never imagined anything like this! Captain Pearson?" said he, imperiously. "Where is he?"

"Here, my Lord," said Pearson, mournfully, coming out of the cabin, where he had withdrawn a little.

"I congratulate you, sir, on —"

"Stop, sir!" cried the captain, in great agony. "You do not understand. This ship — we were not successful."

"What!" cried the admiral. "Is not this the Serapis?"

"Ay, but she belongs—"

"To the Navy of the United States, sir," said a calm voice at his elbow, which made him start; "and she is now commanded by Captain John Paul Jones, at your service. I shall be glad to supply you with a yard-arm, if you have need of one, my Lord—"

"Good God!" said the old man, turning to Jones. "And the Richard?"

"We sunk her, sir," answered Pearson, "but it was useless."

"You have done well, Captain Pearson," said the admiral. "Here is evidence of the fight you made. Never fear; you shall receive reward. 'Twas a defeat as noble as a capture."

"Ay," said Captain Jones, "I can bear witness to the desperate nature of the resistance. "'Twas such as I have never met before in twenty battles on the sea."

"Pearson—my—my—son—" said the admiral, huskily. "How did he bear himself in the fight?"

"Well and nobly, sir, as I can testify," added Pearson.

"I, too," said Jones,—"I saw him. 'Twas he who led your boarders, Captain Pearson, when they tried to sweep our decks."

"And is he well?" said the old admiral, striving to school himself into composure. "That charge, you know, Pearson; I think we need not press it now?" he added.

NOT GUILTY, MY LORD

"No, not now, nor ever, sir," said Pearson, mournfully. "Compose yourself, my dear admiral; he —"

"I am a veteran," said the admiral. "I have looked death in the face for fifty years. Speak plainly. You would say that he is dead."

"Not yet, sir," answered Jones, gently.

"Where is he? Take me to him!"

"He lies aft there on the quarter-deck, sir."

The little group around the dying man made way for the old admiral. He knelt down on the deck opposite Elizabeth, not heeding the others, and gazed long and earnestly in the face of the dying officer.

"The last of his line," he murmured, "and he is gone!" A single tear trickled down the weather-beaten cheek, and splashed upon the face of the young man. "Will he live to know me, think you?" said the admiral, simply, to the surgeon.

"I think so, yes," replied the physician. As if he had heard the question, Coventry opened his eyes; there was recognition in them.

"Father," he murmured faintly.

"My boy — my boy," said the admiral, bowing his head, and striving, manlike, but in vain, to conceal his emotion.

"You told me — not to see you — again; I tried to obey," said Coventry, faintly. "The charge —"

"It is withdrawn; I dismiss it. You have done nobly, Captain Pearson says, and fought like a hero. You are forgiven. I commend you," said the old man, catching his other hand.

"Ah, so," said Coventry, smiling wearily. "Now I must go."

"Not yet!" cried the admiral.

"I — my Lord — " said the young man, wandering again, "may it please the court — may it please the court — " He struggled for breath. "Lift me up," he said.

"'T will be his end," said the doctor, lifting a warning finger.

"Lift me up," cried the dying man, more strongly than before. The admiral nodded. The young Irishman lifted him a little.

"Higher!" he cried. O'Neill lifted him to a sitting position.

"Not guilty, my Lord!" said the young man, resolutely, in a loud, clear voice, throwing his arms out before him, and still smiling. The blood gushed from his lips; and when they laid him back, his plea was heard in that higher court before which the rich and the poor must all finally appear, before which the admiral and the sailor equally must plead.

"*The Lord gave, and the Lord hath taken away; blessed be the name of the Lord,*" said the chaplain of the Serapis, reverently. The men stood around him in a silence broken only by the woman's sobs.

"He has died like a hero, sir," said Jones at last, removing his hat, "and I venture to say that no one of his gallant race, in all the years of their history, has ever made a better end."

"Ah," said the admiral, rising, and mournfully regarding the little group, Elizabeth praying by the

Trieste Publishing has a massive catalogue of classic book titles. Our aim is to provide readers with the highest quality reproductions of fiction and non-fiction literature that has stood the test of time. The many thousands of books in our collection have been sourced from libraries and private collections around the world.

The titles that Trieste Publishing has chosen to be part of the collection have been scanned to simulate the original. Our readers see the books the same way that their first readers did decades or a hundred or more years ago. Books from that period are often spoiled by imperfections that did not exist in the original. Imperfections could be in the form of blurred text, photographs, or missing pages. It is highly unlikely that this would occur with one of our books. Our extensive quality control ensures that the readers of Trieste Publishing's books will be delighted with their purchase. Our staff has thoroughly reviewed every page of all the books in the collection, repairing, or if necessary, rejecting titles that are not of the highest quality. This process ensures that the reader of one of Trieste Publishing's titles receives a volume that faithfully reproduces the original, and to the maximum degree possible, gives them the experience of owning the original work.

We pride ourselves on not only creating a pathway to an extensive reservoir of books of the finest quality, but also providing value to every one of our readers. Generally, Trieste books are purchased singly - on demand, however they may also be purchased in bulk. Readers interested in bulk purchases are invited to contact us directly to enquire about our tailored bulk rates. Email: customerservice@triestepublishing.com

You May Also Like

ISBN: 9780649731213
Paperback: 160 pages
Dimensions: 6.14 x 0.34 x 9.21 inches
Language: eng

War Poems, 1898

California Club & Irving M. Scott

ISBN: 9780649587667
Paperback: 176 pages
Dimensions: 6.14 x 0.38 x 9.21 inches
Language: eng

Second Year Language Reader

Franklin T. Baker & George R. Carpenter & Katharine B. Owen

www.triestepublishing.com

You May Also Like

Report of the Second Annual Meeting of the Maryland State Bar Association, Held at Ocean City, Maryland, July 28-29, 1897

Conway W. Sams

ISBN: 9780649724185
Paperback: 130 pages
Dimensions: 6.14 x 0.28 x 9.21 inches
Language: eng

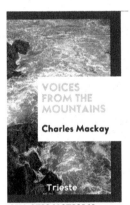

Voices from the Mountains

Charles Mackay

ISBN: 9780649730360
Paperback: 140 pages
Dimensions: 5.25 x 0.30 x 8.0 inches
Language: eng

www.triestepublishing.com

You May Also Like

ISBN: 9780649420544
Paperback: 108 pages
Dimensions: 6.14 x 0.22 x 9.21 inches
Language: eng

1807-1907 The One Hundredth Anniversary of the incorporation of the Town of Arlington Massachusetts

Various

ISBN: 9780649194292
Paperback: 44 pages
Dimensions: 6.14 x 0.09 x 9.21 inches
Language: eng

Biennial report of the Board of State Harbor Commissioners, for the two fiscal years commencing July 1, 1890, and ending June 30, 1892

Various

www.triestepublishing.com

You May Also Like

Biennial report of the Board of State Harbor Commissioners for the two fisca years. Commeneing July 1, 1884, and Ending June 30, 1886

Various

ISBN: 9780649199693
Paperback: 48 pages
Dimensions: 6.14 x 0.10 x 9.21 inches
Language: eng

Biennial report of the Board of state commissioners, for the two fiscal years, commencing July 1, 1890, and ending June 30, 1892

Various

ISBN: 9780649196395
Paperback: 44 pages
Dimensions: 6.14 x 0.09 x 9.21 inches
Language: eng

Find more of our titles on our website. We have a selection of thousands of titles that will interest you. Please visit

www.triestepublishing.com

Lightning Source UK Ltd.
Milton Keynes UK
UKOW06f1459231017
311488UK00007B/1601/P